The
TEACHING
of the
MASTER

Foundation for
Christian Living

Nadia G. Boctor

Copyright © 2010 by Nadia G. Boctor

The Teaching of the Master
by Nadia G. Boctor

Printed in the United States of America

ISBN 9781615798919

All rights reserved solely by the author. The author guarantees all contents are original and do not infringe upon the legal rights of any other person or work. No part of this book may be reproduced in any form without the permission of the author. The views expressed in this book are not necessarily those of the publisher.

All Scripture quotations, unless otherwise noted, are taken from the *Holy Bible: New International Version* (North American Edition). Copyright @ 1978, by the International Bible Society. Used by permission of Zondervan, without the prior permission of the publisher.

Edited by Freddy Boutros
Cover Design by Freddy Boutros

www.xulonpress.com

Table of Contents

Acknowledgement vii
Introduction ix

Part I- About the Master Teacher 13

Chapter 1   Understanding God's Purpose for Mankind 15
Chapter 2   The Person of Jesus 28
Chapter 3   The Message of the Master 47
Chapter 4   The Master's Teaching Methods 65

Part II- Effectiveness of the Master's Teaching 81

Chapter 5   Permanent Change 83
Chapter 6   A New Life 94
Chapter 7   Blessed Assurance 106
Chapter 8   The Matchless Friend 117

Part III - Applications of the Master's Teaching 127

Chapter 9   Continued Fellowship 129
Chapter 10   Personal Growth 139
Chapter 11   Sharing the Gospel 148
Chapter 12   Accomplished Mission 156

Bibliography 165
Endnotes 169
General Index 177

Acknowledgement

"......you have ten thousand instructors in Christ" (1Cor 4:15a).

I am most of all grateful to my Lord and Savior Jesus Christ, who inspired, strengthened, and gave me the desire to share with my readers His tremendously effective teaching.

Many people have greatly helped me in preparing this study and I wish to thank them all. I acknowledge with thanks the support of Dr. Milad Philopos, Professor at the International Bible College and Seminary in Independence, Missouri. He has been my advising professor and mentor throughout my Biblical Studies at this university, and has shared in my zeal for this work.

Special thanks go to Rev. Latif Fahim Marcos, Pastor of the Arabic Bible Christian Church in Long Beach California- a beacon of the Christian faith- for his ongoing teaching which is inspired by the Holy Spirit and which has become indispensable to many Arabic-speaking men and women. And many thanks go to Wedad Khalil for all her assistance.

I am deeply indebted to my family, especially my husband, Robert, our son Ragi, and to our granddaughters Lorine, Jizelle and Valerie, and to Amy, and to all my friends who have been patient with me while I worked on my studies, and who have encouraged and supported me in all my endeavors.

Introduction

"The Jews were amazed and asked, 'How did this man get such learning, without having studied?'" (Jn 7:15).

Although He had no formal education that we know of, writers, scholars and theologians have frequently referred to Jesus as the 'Master Teacher.'

Jesus preferred to be called 'Teacher,' and He often used this title when referring to Himself! This fact certainly bestows honor on whomsoever chooses teaching as a profession—on all of us who have an innate passion for teaching.

There are times in the life span of every individual, when that person plays the role of a teacher. Parents are constantly teaching their children. They do it as a free will act of love. Their goal is to have their children grow-physically, intellectually and emotionally, and ultimately succeed in life by developing a good understanding of the world in which they live. Older siblings teach the younger ones. Supervisors guide and teach their subordinates. A good schoolteacher is devoted to helping each student acquire the knowledge needed to succeed and proceed to the next grade level, and eventually to graduate, get a job and make a living. A good teacher sets goals for the students, strives to have the students reach them, and is extremely proud when they do attain, or exceed those goals.

The teachings of Jesus are the basis for the Christian doctrine upon which the Christian faith was built, and has survived and flourished throughout the ages. Without this divine teaching and the everlasting blessings that ensued, man's life on this earth would have been useless. In the 'School of Jesus', millions of people from different cultures and backgrounds have for two thousand years learned the principles of living the true Christian life and have put them to practice. The Master's words were, and still are, able to put people on the right track in their relationships, both with God and with their fellow men. His teaching is not a random combination of abstract ideas and words, but is the source of the power, which still transforms the lives of men and women to this day.

But before one enlists in the 'School of Jesus', one must first consider the reasons that make Jesus, the 'Master Teacher,' different from all other teachers and rabbis. One should consider the reasons that rendered the crowds amazed at His teaching. Furthermore, one has to look for the reasons that made His enemies, as well as His followers, testify to His great teaching.

The Teaching of the Master

Because He is God the Son, His message is divine and taught with authority! Since He is the incarnate God, He has outshined all scholars, prophets and philosophers in His time on earth and ever after. Jesus' teaching had one main purpose: to tell the story of God's love and sacrifice for humankind. His teaching still leads people to repentance and to regaining fellowship with God, thus fulfilling God's purpose in creating us. We marvel at God's work through these teachings as we see more and more people come to a saving faith in Him.

This study will highlight the tools Jesus used to change the lives of people in His audiences throughout history, thus fulfilling God's purpose in sending Him to our earth. In analyzing the Master's teaching, one comes to the realization that these are 'model teachings' which will never wane or become obsolete or out-dated. His word will remain alive and effective for evermore.

The Holy Bible, especially the four gospels, will be used as the main source of information. Part One, will present a close up study "About the Master Teacher' of *'Who'* Jesus—the person—was, *'What'* He taught, and *'How'* He did it. In Part Two, the study will focus on the Effectiveness of the Master's Teaching' in our daily lives. Part Three provides 'Applications of the Master's Teaching', and discusses our duty as Christians to continue in fellowship with Him and be nourished by Him in order to grow, to share the gospel with others, and to fulfill the 'Great Commission' He gave His disciples and consequently all of us.

Part I

About the Master Teacher

Chapter 1

Understanding God's Purpose for Mankind

"...For he chose us in him before the creation of the world to be holy and blameless in his sight. In love he predestined us to be adopted as his sons through Jesus Christ, in accordance with his pleasure and will" (Eph 1: 4-5).

This chapter examines God's purpose for creating humankind, and how that purpose transcended through the teaching of the Master. Eventually this will lead us to understand the necessary steps to fulfill our duties and to carry out our responsibilities in response to God's purpose in creating us.

God has used many methods to communicate with us. He spoke directly with Adam and Eve. He spoke to some people through revelations and dreams. With others, He used signs. In the Old Testament, God gave messages to people through His prophets.

More than two thousand years ago, God sent His only begotten Son to speak to us and to explain God's purpose for creating us. In that respect, Irving Jensen[1] wrote, "The person of Jesus is the key to all history. He is the Messiah who had been in God's plan before the creation of the world."

God's primary purpose in creating us is to share the joy of His gracious love. In creating us, God wants to satisfy His glory and goodness. Secondly, God's purpose is to *increase* His joy by sharing the Trinity in creation and redemption. The third purpose is that He wants us to fulfill our duties by worshipping Him as well as ministering to others about Him.

The first purpose of God in creating us is to make us share the joy of His gracious love. In order for that process to get started, God created us in His image. He chose Israel as a nation to reflect that image and He set some objectives for His nation. Daniel Fuller[2] stated that God freely created us out of love, and He wants the best for us. He wrote:

> God created us in the freedom of his benevolent love, out of mercy and grace... God in his benevolent love towards creation wants to serve the very best interests of as many people as possible. God says, 'I will rejoice in doing them good and will assuredly plant them in this land with all my heart and soul' (Jer 32:41).

Man sinned against God in spite of His graciousness. This disobedience caused a separation that did not meet the criteria of God's purpose and man had to pay for the wages of sin in eternal hell. Therefore, in order for us to be saved and to be able to enjoy eternal life, the Father, in His benevolent love, sent us His Son with great tidings: The kingdom of God is at hand! He explained to us what God's love is and the purpose He had for us. He taught us the ethics of the kingdom. He showed us the way and led us with love and compassion to understand God's purpose for us.

The Apostle John points out that since no one has seen the Father except the Son, He, the Son, is the only one who can explain to us the kingdom of heaven through His teaching. He can enlighten our minds and hearts and prepare us to live with Him through the Triune. The Scripture says,

> No one has ever seen God, but God the only Son, who is at the Father's side, has made him [the Father] known (Jn 1:18).

The Gospel of Mark documents that Jesus went to pray early in the morning in a solitary place. Simon Peter, His disciple, went with his companions to look for Him. When they found Him, they exclaimed, "Everyone is looking for you!" Jesus replied,

> Let us go somewhere else—to the nearby villages—so I can preach there also. This is why I have come (Mk 1:37-38).

The Master Teacher demonstrated for us God's love in practice. In His teaching, He summed up God's purpose for humankind in the Golden Rule that consists of two commandments. (Mk 12:30-31).

The *first* commandment is "Love the Lord your God". It was quoted abundantly in the Scripture: Deut 6:5; Mt 22:37; Mk 12:30; Lk 10:27. This commandment motivates us to look up to God for the pleasure and happiness that He has set forth in front of us. Since the Lord is One, He alone can satisfy that happiness, because He created us in His own image. It is true that with the sin of our ancestor, Adam, we are all born in sin, yet, God in His graciousness has kept His promises to us. We can always change our future, if we love Him with all our heart, soul and strength.

The *second* commandment is "Love your neighbor as yourself". It was quoted frequently as well: Lev 16:18; Mt 5:43, 19:19, 13:39; Mk 12:31; Lk 10:27; Rom 13:9; Gal 5:14; Js 2:8. This commandment comes as the result of the first commandment. If we love God, it is our duty and joy to share that love with our neighbors, regardless of whom or what they are.

To love your neighbor as yourself is another way of demonstrating your love to God. Jesus also added in the same verse in Mark, "There is no commandment greater than these." Both Islam and Buddhism preach on helping one's neighbor in time of need. Yet, only Christianity puts neighbor as oneself. Jesus further explained this commandment in another teaching session when He said, "In everything, do to others what you would have them do to you, for this sums up the law and the prophets" (Mt 7:12). The Master urges us to do so because we have been created in God's image, likewise is our neighbor. If we hurt another person, we hurt God.

Jesus presented the two parts of the Golden Rule as one and interrelated; each part is indispensable of the other. If we choose to love God and satisfy our need for love, that love will create in us a positive attitude to help and love others, and not hurt them by word or deed. Knowing God for who He is simultaneously urges us to love others as ourselves. We have in the Father and the Son the love that extends to all people, regardless of their faith, color, language, age, race, gender, marital status, background, educational and economic status, physical or mental ability. God does not hate or seek revenge on sinners. The words 'avenge' and 'revenge' were used in the Old Testament only to denote God's justice towards those who try to hurt His people. The Scripture declares in an oracle concerning Nineveh:

> The Lord is a jealous and avenging God; the Lord takes vengeance and is filled with wrath (Nah 1:2).

The New Testament emphasizes God's zeal towards His people, by saying,

> And will not God bring about justice to his own chosen ones, who cry out to him day and night? (Lk 18:7).

One of the stunning fulfillments of the Law that Jesus stated was "Love your enemies" (Mt 5:44; Lk 6:27, 35). God's love is unique, indispensable and unlike any other love. Even if an enemy is not doing God's will, God still loves that person.

The disciples of Jesus experienced the joy of first-hand love being in the presence of Jesus for three years. They had the joy to walk alongside God, whose greatest delight comes in sharing His supreme happiness with those who turn the control of their lives over to Him. In the Gospel of John, Jesus teaches us:

> Whoever has my commands and obeys them, he is the one who loves me. He who loves me will be loved by my Father, and I too will love him, and show myself to him (Jn 14: 21).

Daniel Fuller[3] adds:

> We should therefore delight ourselves in God to satisfy our need-love. Then we want to increase our joy looking for him to satisfy our joy by exercising benevolent love to all other people.

Secondly, God's purpose in creation is to *increase* our joy by sharing with us the unity of being a Triune God: the Father, the Son and the Holy Spirit. The Son of God, the Master Teacher and Savior is the embodiment of God. The Holy Spirit is the embodiment of the joy the Father and the Son have in each other. As God created us in His own image, He shaped us in such a way that we can receive the Holy Spirit, if we submit our lives to the Father in the name of the Son. Jesus and the Holy Spirit existed side by side with God before God created the universe. In Genesis, God used the plural form when He was about to create Adam, by saying (Italics are used for clarification):

> Let *us* make man in *our* image, in *our* likeness, and let them rule over the fish of the sea and the birds of the air, over the livestock, over all the earth ….." (Gen 1:26).

Jesus clearly stated that He existed before creation. The Gospel of John declares this fact on the onset (Italics are used for clarification):

> In the beginning was the *Word*, and the *Word* was with God, and the *Word* was God. *He* was with God *in the beginning*. Through *him* all things were made that has been made (Jn 1:1-3*a*).

Jesus also explained His unity with the Father. He said,

> For as the Father has life in himself, so he granted the Son to have life in himself. And he has given him authority to judge because he is the Son of Man (Jn 5:26-27).

As for the Holy Spirit, Genesis 1:2 declares (Italics are used for clarification):

> Now the earth was formless and empty, darkness was over the surface of the deep, and *the Spirit of God* was hovering over the waters.

Jesus announced the future outpour of the Holy Spirit to His disciples after they showed great despair when He told them He would no longer be with them. He promised them [us] that when He would go back to heaven, He would soon send the Spirit of Comfort. Not long after His ascension, the new church members were filled with the Holy Spirit.

Matt Freidman[4] brings about an interesting analysis of God's objectives for Israel that consists of three dimensions. The first dimension is that God's nation, Israel, would be a nation that is morally pure, and would mirror His holiness through Christ. Secondly, Freidman assures that service will emerge from the holy character, as manifested in the second commandment to love one's neighbor as oneself. Thirdly, the holy character and the service would be communicated to spread the message of truth about God's kingdom. He points out:

> [God] desires his people to reflect him as individuals within a unified body. God wanted his people in community because he is community-Three in One. Intimacy among God's people is a reflection of him.

God's purpose is to save us from eternal hell. That is the main reason why He sent His Son to earth. Through His divine teaching, Jesus taught us the ethics of the kingdom and explained to us God's love and mercy. He offered His life as a sacrifice for our redemption. He died on the cross in order to deliver us from eternal death. The Book of Esther in the Old Testament tells us the story of great love and sacrifice. The book is loaded with cons and pros: love and hate, reward and revenge, sacrifice and selfishness. The key persons in the book are Esther, Mordecai, King Xerxes and Haman. Although the poor Jewish orphan Hadassah [Esther] became a queen after she married the Gentile King Xerxes, she had a strong urge to sacrifice her position as queen to save her people, the Jews, from being wiped out, through the intrigues of Haman, the second man in the kingdom. She could have disclosed those intrigues to her husband, the king, and asked him for revenge. Yet, she chose to rescue her race and leave revenge to God. However, one can wonder if what she did for her people would be equivalent to what she would have done if those people were not Jews. Would she have undertaken the same risk? Yet the Master took the risk on the cross based on His love to each and every person. He offers His love based on one condition: each person should readily surrender his or her life to God's purpose, ultimately resulting in a radical change in one's life. Before He ascended to heaven, Jesus promised to come and take us to live with Him if we fulfill God's purpose on earth.

Furthermore, we should take action to demonstrate our love to God because in His defined purpose, He promised that if we follow Him, He guarantees our future, on earth as well as in heaven. Everything on earth will fade away; nothing on earth is everlasting. Yet, God's purpose never changes. He cares for each one of us. He feeds the sparrows and likewise He takes care of the minutes of our lives. He has an answer to all our inquiries and He can silence all our anxieties.

Jesus loves sinners and rejoices when any one of them is saved.

In the parable of 'The Lost Sheep' Jesus describes the joy of the shepherd when he finds the lost sheep, saying:

> And if he finds it, I tell you the truth, he is happier about that one sheep than the ninety-nine sheep that did not wander off. In the same way your Father in heaven is not willing that any of these little ones [the least] should be lost (Mt 18:13-14).

Thirdly, God's purpose for humankind is that we fulfill our duties by worshipping Him and submitting our lives to Him. That will lead us to minister to others about Him. There are two main steps in submitting to God's purpose:

Step One is to believe that He is the Triune God.

Our Duty is to have fellowship with the Triune God (First Commandment).

Step Two is to recognize God's offer of love to the whole world.

Our Duty is to return God's love to us by loving Him, as well as extending our love to others (Second Commandment). We can manage to do that by devoting our time, hearts and abilities towards helping others to minister that God alone can change one's life. Therefore, believers can all be more and more like Jesus. Just as a cell multiplies, we Christians can spread God's free love by ministering to others.

The Master Teacher explained to His disciples the outcome of fulfilling God's purpose. He said,

> When the Son of Man comes in his glory and all the angels with him, he will sit on his throne, in heavenly glory. All the nations will be gathered before him, and he will separate the people one from another...Then the king will say to those on the right 'come you who are blessed by my Father, take your inheritance in the kingdom prepared for you since the creation of the world' (Mt 25:31-34).

Since the wages of sin is death, Jesus has paid the price on the cross. In order to be worthy to live with Him forever, He explained to us through His teaching the ethics of the kingdom. Knowing that God has a defined purpose for humankind, it is our duty to take action that reflects His love. In other words, we have to demonstrate our love to Him. Moreover, the second part of the Golden Rule in Mark 12:31 demands from us to demonstrate our love to others, as we should do to ourselves. That is a natural outcome of the first part of the Golden Rule.

In order to fulfill God's purpose, it is necessary to follow the footsteps of Jesus. Studying the Scripture and believing the truth of God's purpose therein will result in productive ministry that leads others to Christ. In the Book of Acts, Paul gives an impressive farewell speech to the Ephesians (Acts 20: 20-35). He sums up God's purpose by saying:

> For I have not hesitated to proclaim to you the whole *will* of God (v. 27).

Paul urges the Ephesians to:
  a. repent (v. 21),
  b. be shepherds (v. 28-29),
  c. be watchful (v. 28),
  d. inherit God's grace (v. 32),
  e. follow His model as Christians (v. 35), and

    f. give to the needy (v. 35).

To sum up, God's purpose is that all humankind be saved. In order to fulfill God's purpose, we have to obey His commandments, search the Scripture, recognize His voice and surrender all to Him. What God yearns for, is that our prayers should be lifted up to Him, as an incense of our love and thanksgiving. Other people should be able to see the light of God in our deeds in order to follow Him. Accepting Jesus as Master and Lord is essential to each individual's salvation. It is through the unity of the church that members in the body of Christ become stronger, and work in a purposeful ministry that transforms lives.

Chapter 2

The Person of Jesus

"Take my yoke upon you and learn from me, for I am gentle and humble in heart, and you will find rest for your souls" (Mt 11:29).

More than two thousand years ago, God sent His Son Jesus Christ to our planet. His birth was expected, because Isaiah, as well as many other prophets, had prophesied of His coming.

> Therefore, the Lord himself will give you a sign: The virgin will be with child and will give birth to a son, and will call him Immanuel (Isa 7:14; Mt 1:23).

Another prophecy of Isaiah confirmed the birth of Jesus and described Him more specifically:

> For to us a child is born, to us a son is given, and the government will be on his shoulders. And he will be called Wonderful Counselor, Mighty God, Everlasting Father, Prince of Peace. Of the increase of his government and peace, there will be no end. He will reign on David's throne and over his kingdom, establishing and upholding it with justice and righteousness from that time on and forever. The zeal of the Lord Almighty will accomplish this (Isa 9:6-7).

The angel of the Lord brought two tidings to Virgin Mary that she would be the Mother of the Savior, as well as the news that the elderly couple, Elisabeth and Zechariah, would have a son. The first chapter of the Gospel of Luke documents the spiritual Song of Zechariah who said:

> And you my child [John], will be called a prophet of the Most High, for you will go on before the Lord to prepare the way for him, to give the people the knowledge of salvation, through the forgiveness of their sins, because of the tender mercy of our God, by which the rising sun will come to us from heaven to shine on those living in darkness and in the shadow of death, to guide our feet into the path of peace (Lk 1:76-79).

Jesus' Birth

When He was born, the host of angels sang, "Glory to God in the highest, and on earth peace to men on whom his favor rests" (Lk 2:14). In fact, we learn from the Scripture that Jesus had existed from the beginning. In the first chapter of the Gospel of John we read, "He was in the world, and though the world was made through him, the world did not recognize him" (Jn 1:10).

Jesus' Early Years

Although the three gospels document Jesus' birth, we know little about Him until the age of twelve. The Scripture tells us that at that age Jesus had developed in wisdom as well as in stature (Lk 2:52). We learn also that at that age, He sat in the temple courts with the rabbis, and took part in their discussions. Once, He had stayed behind in the temple and His parents returned to look for Him. The Scripture tells us:

> After three days, they [his parents] found him in the temple courts, sitting among the teachers, listening to them and asking them questions. Everyone who heard him was amazed at his understanding and answers (Lk 2:46).

We also learn that on that same incident, He challenged His parent's worry, "'Why were you searching for me?' he asked. 'Didn't you know I had to be in my Father's house?' But they did not understand what he was saying to them" (Lk 2:49).

Jesus' business and main concern at the age of twelve was to educate teachers (rabbis) about God, the Father, about Himself and about the Holy Spirit. No wonder, He grew to be the Master Teacher.

Before Jesus started His ministry on earth, He had a clash with Satan. He crushed Satan and won victory. That victory made a crucial change in our lives.

How did Jesus describe Himself?

Jesus described Himself in the well-known verses starting with 'I am'. He said (Bold font is used for clarification):

"**I am** the light of the world. Whoever follows me will never walk in darkness" (Jn 8:12*b*).

"**I am** the good shepherd. The good shepherd lays down his life for the sheep" (Jn 10:11).

"**I am** the way and the truth and the life. No one comes to the Father except through me" (Jn 14:6*b*).

"**I am** the true vine and my Father is the gardener" (Jn 15:1).

"**I am** the living bread that came down from heaven" (Jn 6:51*a*).

"**I am** the gate: whoever enters through me will be saved" (Jn 10:9*a*).

The Characteristics of the Master Teacher's Personality

He carries a human as well as a divine personality. He shows us the image of God. He is kind, modest, compassionate, loving, merciful and forgiving. He taught us God's wisdom and laws through His words and deeds. He taught us love, mercy and compassion. Through His healing power, He healed the blind, the lame, the afflicted and the demon-possessed. He even brought the dead to life. He taught everywhere and at any time: He taught in the temple in Jerusalem, in synagogues, in open fields, on ships, on the mountain, near a well and in homes.

Jesus the Incarnate God

Jesus is God, who has the power to heal and to resurrect from the dead. He performed astounding miracles: "[He] healed all the sick" (Mt 8:16*b*).

David McKenna[6] discussed the 'Incarnate character' of the Master. He wrote:

> The incarnation of Jesus Christ is the Pivot upon which our world turns. Whether to understand his life or his leadership, we must begin with the incarnation. Then, from the mystery of its paradox and the miracle of its resolution, the meaning of the "word became flesh" unfolds before us. From his incarnate character, we learn the meaning of his redemptive vision, his servant strategy and his teaching task.

Warren Benson[5] describes Him as the God-Man:

> Jesus of Nazareth was the true Messiah of his people (John 1:41; Rom 9:5) who was anointed with the Spirit and power (Acts 10:38). He was the true prophet (Mk 9:7), priest (John 17), and king (Matt 2:2, 21:5). Orthodox Christians of every church and denomination have perennially insisted that Jesus Christ rose from the dead (1Cor 15) and that this doctrinal belief is a cornerstone of the New Testament faith. Christianity IS Jesus Christ, who was both God and man. He is the second Person of the Trinity. His death on the cross provides perfect sinless sacrifice for our redemption, the forgiveness of sin being available to those who by faith receive the gift of salvation.

The Master once asked His disciples:

> 'Who do people say the Son of Man is?' They replied, 'Some say John the Baptist, others say Elijah; and still others, Jeremiah or one of the prophets'. 'But what about you?' He asked, 'Who do you say I am?' Simon Peter answered, 'You are Jesus the Christ, Son of the living God' (Mt 16:13*b*-15).

Jesus the Servant

Jesus came as a servant. He said, "......whoever wants to become great among you must be your servant, and whoever wants to be first must be your slave - Just as the Son of Man did not come to be served, but to serve, and to give his life as a ransom for many" (Mt 20: 26b-28).

Jesus the King

Jesus is the King of kings. When He entered Jerusalem before the Passover He was welcomed as a king. People lay their clothes and palm leaves on the ground to welcome Him (Jn 12:12-15). On His second coming, He will judge the whole world (Mt 25: 31-46).

Teacher and Rabbi

He is a teacher and rabbi. He spent His brief life as a wandering teacher working, more or less, in a remote corner of the Roman Empire, which was in control of Israel at the time. We can also learn more about His personality as a teacher if we make a close-up study of His disciples. His twelve disciples were ordinary men; most of them were in the trade of fishing. They accompanied Him almost all the time. Hence, they had hands-on training. One of the duties of any master teacher, in general, is to train junior teachers, because those methods are usually emulated as the standard. In the disciples' case, their Master Teacher was God in person. Elton Trueblood[7] summarized the philosophy of the Master that shaped His teaching method concerning His disciples. He stated:

> It is no exaggeration to say that Christ's decision to select the twelve was one of the most crucial decisions of the world.

> There is no reason to suppose that we should have ever heard the gospel apart from this carefully conceived step. Since Christ wrote no book, he depended entirely upon the faithful men of the prepared group. Not all of them understood him nor proved faithful. Yet in the end, the method succeeded.

Jesus not only inspired His disciples, He is the model on which people from all kinds build their lives. He is the source of inspiration to all nations. Matt Freidman[8] gives more insight in that regard:

> Perhaps the most powerful evidence for Jesus as educator is the entourage of disciples that accompanied him. The disciples-literally "learners"-were a community of interested persons, who saw in Jesus not only a speaker of memorable ability, but also a model of righteous living. As a mentor, Jesus opened up to those people not only his words but his entire life.

Furthermore, we can learn about the Master Teacher when we come closer to His audience. Besides the twelve, the thousands that followed Him and listened to Him were homogeneous. Those who benefited from His teaching were ordinary men and women: Pharisees, Scribes, rabbis, Sadducees, military and religious leaders. They were a mix of the Jews and the Gentiles, the poor and the rich, the sick and the healthy, the clean and the unclean. Those people represented many cultures, backgrounds and beliefs. Believers and sinners came in droves to Him because of who He was and how He taught them. People were amazed at His teaching, which was divine and not like the teaching of the Scribes. To those who chose to follow Him, He gave them a new life on earth, and an assurance of eternal life with Him in heaven. Yet, others hated Him.

The people who hated Him, falsely accused Him and collaborated to crucify Him. One of the reasons they did so was because He confronted them with their hypocrisy and evil deeds. Yet, the number of Jesus' listeners when He was on earth varied from one person to over five thousand. Although Jesus had twelve designated disciples, He accepted, and still accepts all believers in His name to become His disciples.

Man of Justice

One more aspect we learn about the person of Jesus is His equality. He treated all people equally: Jews and Gentiles, men and women, children and adults, poor and rich, sick and healthy, believers and sinners. All were treated the same and loved equally. Not only did He associate with sinners, but He also promised that He would seat the least of people on earth on twelve thrones, so that they may judge the tribes of Israel (Mt 19:28). Luke reported:

> Now the tax-collectors and "sinners" were all gathering around to hear him. But the Pharisees and the teachers of the law muttered 'This man welcomes sinners and eats with them' (Lk 15:1-2).

Man of Modesty

Another great characteristic of the Master Teacher is His modesty. Although He is a king, He is ready to come into our lives. Yet, He wants us to accept Him first, and He will be our sincere friend. When Jesus revealed Himself to John after His ascension, He declared,

> Here I am! I stand at the door and knock. If anyone hears my voice and opens the door, I will come in and eat with him and he with me. To him who overcomes, I will give the right to sit with me on my throne (Rev 3:20-21*a*).

Embodiment of Love

A major characteristic of the Master's personality is His love. Because "God is love" (1Jn 4:16*b*), He demonstrated that love was the main reason He came to earth. He paid His own blood to save us from eternal death. The most memorized verse in the New Testament sums up God's love to us:

> For God so loved the world that he gave his one and only Son, that whoever believes in him shall not perish but have eternal life (John 3:16).

Although the Ten Commandments advocate that we love our neighbors like ourselves, Jesus elevates that love to the highest level. In His 'Sermon on the Mount', Jesus said:

> You have heard that it was said, 'Love your neighbor and hate your enemy.' But I tell you: Love your enemies and pray for those who persecute you, that you may be sons of your Father in heaven. He causes his sun to rise on the evil and the good, and sends rain on the righteous and the unrighteous (Mt 5:43-45).

Attitude toward Sinners

The Master's attitude toward sinners is one of the most beloved qualities of Jesus. He sat, talked and ate with them. He offered them His message of love and forgiveness. When the Pharisees and the Scribes grumbled against Him over such associations, He responded saying:

> I tell you that in the same way there is more rejoicing in heaven over one sinner who repents than over ninety-nine righteous persons who do not need to repent. (Lk 15:7).

Man of Compassion

Jesus did not only uplift the souls of His listeners who came to hear Him, He healed their diseases and shared their sorrows. The Scripture documents that He raised from the dead (Jn 11:38-44).

King of Peace

When Jesus was born, He brought peace on earth. Before His crucifixion, resurrection and ascension, Jesus wanted to comfort His disciples who were sad when they learned that He would soon not be with them. He said to them:

> Peace I leave with you, my peace I give unto you. I do not give to you as the world gives. Do not let your hearts be troubled and do not be afraid (Jn 14:27).

The peace that fills the hearts of Christians when they accept Jesus into their lives should not be confused with what Jesus meant when He said:

> I have come to bring fire on the earth, and I wish it were already kindled! But I have a baptism to undergo, and how distressed I am until it is completed! Do you think I came to bring peace on earth? No, I tell you, but division (Lk 12:49-51).

Jesus meant that the world would be split on whether to worship Jesus or the devil. We can see that that prophecy is being fulfilled in our days.

Jesus' main concern while on earth was to spread His message of peace to all humankind, in order for them to know Him for who He was and not what they wanted Him to be. Nevertheless, the Messiah that the Jews had expected, or what their souls aspired for, was a king, who would lift them up from the yoke of foreign rule by the Romans, whereas, the Messiah who came to earth was a poor man in ragged clothes who sprang from the poor Galilee surroundings. He did not have a place to lay His head (Lk 9:58), and His father, Joseph, was a carpenter. He had no formal education, and He certainly did not fit with what the Jews had expected. Hence, some of the rigid Jews did not accept His message. But Jesus did not stand still towards their speculation, doubt, persecution and hatred. He was confrontational, and addressed their refusal to accept Him. In some encounters, He called them "hypocrites" (Mt 6:5; Mk 7:6; Lk 6:42). When He spoke of the 'seven woes', He said:

> You snakes! You brood of vipers! How will you escape being condemned to hell? (Mt 23:33).

Man of Fulfillment

Jesus' personality and actions were in accordance with the Law. His teaching was the fulfillment of the Law. Yet, in some instances,

Jesus' adversaries mistakenly perceived His actions and teachings as contradictory to the Law. He addressed their speculation in the 'Sermon on the Mount' by saying that He had not come to abolish the Law but to fulfill it. Jesus promised before His ascension to send the Holy Spirit, the Spirit of Comfort, and He fulfilled His promise. Soon after He ascended to heaven, He sent the Holy Spirit to empower and guide believers on earth, until His second coming. He is the unseen God whose words are true forever.

Man of Suffering

Jesus' suffering on earth was foretold many centuries before His birth through God-sent prophets. Jesus' suffering throughout His ministry, as well as His arrest, trial and death, continue to be shocking. The good news is that He overcame death when God raised Him from the dead on the third day.

Jesus' suffering started as soon as He began His mission on earth. The Jewish rulers always pointed their sinful arrows against Him. Yet, His crucifixion surfaces more often than any suffering Jesus experienced. The fact remains that His suffering on earth is a mirror of what happens to Christians for the faith: persecution, despise, rejection, torture and death for the name of Christ.

Looking deeply into Jesus' suffering, before His crucifixion, gives solace and comfort to His followers as Jesus always surrendered to the Father's will. When He entered Gethsemane, He was sad, yet He came out of Gethsemane with power and peace because He surrendered to the Father's will.

We can learn about who Jesus was when we study His arrest and trial more closely (Lk 22-23:44). Luke documents the satanic plot to betray Jesus (22:1-2); the last sad hours of Jesus' life with the disciples (22:7-46); the cruel scorn hurled against Him by the religious leaders and the mob they had incited (22:47; 23:25); and the agony of scourging and crucifixion (23:26-44). Jesus' arrest took place by the Jewish religious leaders who had plotted for that arrest long before its execution. Irving Jensen[9] points out the account of the trial as one of the darkest episodes in Jesus' life. Mark documents that torture:

> Then some began to spit on him, and blindfolded him, struck him with their fists, and said, 'Prophesy!' And the guards took him and beat him (Mk 14:65).

The trial of Jesus was illegal. He was brought at night, tied with ropes, to the quarters of Annas, the former, non-official High Priest. The Sanhedrin could find nothing to prosecute Him with, yet they put Him on trial. He was tried twice by Pontius Pilate and once by Herod. Herod sent Him back to Pontius Pilate who was not convinced that Jesus deserved death, yet he handed Him to the soldiers to scourge Him. Pilate even allowed them to make a crown of thorns and lay it on His head. Afraid of the people,

Pilate finally delivered Him to the Roman soldiers to crucify Him, with one bandit on His right, and another bandit on His left. The Scripture foretold this suffering:

> He was oppressed and treated harshly. Yet, he never said a word. He was led as a lamb to the slaughter, and as a sheep is silent before its shearer, he did not open his mouth. From prison to trial, they led him away to his death. But who among the people realized that he was dying for their sins-that he was suffering for their punishment? He had done no wrong and he never deceived any one, but he was buried like a criminal. He was put in a rich man's grave (Isa 53:7-9).[10]

Jesus' crucifixion reveals three kinds of pain that the Master had to go through:

Physical Pain: This pain cannot be described in our limited human understanding. Yet, that pain was obvious in Jesus' seven statements on the cross.

Mental Struggle: This struggle was caused because of the physical struggle. Jesus was torn between His duty to carry on His mission and the agony of crucifixion.

Spiritual Agony: Jesus was on the cross, suffering from severe physical agony and mental pain, but more severe was the emotional and spiritual pain. He was struggling with the thoughts concerning the sins of the world for which He had come. He knew that redemption was the core of His mission, and that He had to go through that painful struggle in order that His mission would be 'finished' on the cross.

Now, that we have familiarized ourselves with who the person of Jesus is, one gets more curious to know Jesus, the person, when He comes again. The Apostle John was inspired through the Holy Spirit to describe Jesus as he saw Him after His ascension:

> I turned around to see the voice that was speaking to me. And when I turned I saw seven lamp stands and among the lamp stands was someone standing like a son of man, dressed in a robe reaching down to his feet and with a golden sash around his chest. His head and hair were white like wool, as white as snow. And his eyes were like blazing fire. His feet were like bronze glowing in a furnace, and his voice was like the sound of rushing waters. In his right hand, he held seven stars, and out of his mouth came a sharp double-edged sword. His face was like the sun shining in all its brilliance (Rev 1:12-16).

The description of Jesus in the Book of Revelation also reveals Him as the Ruler of all the nations:

> Grace and peace to you from him who is, and who was, and who is to come, and from the seven spirits before his throne, and from Jesus Christ who is the faithful witness, the first-born from the dead, and the ruler of the kings of the earth. To him who loves us and has freed us from our sins by his blood, and has made us to be a kingdom and priests to serve his God and Father (Rev 1:4*b*-6*a*).

Furthermore, many other qualities are attributed to Him in the Book of Revelation. He is described as:

The Alpha and the Omega (1:8)
The Faithful and True Witness (3:14)
The Creator (4:11)
The Lion of Judah (5:5)
King of kings and Lord of all (19:16)
The Bright Morning Star (2:28; 22:16)
The Living One (1:18)
The Son of Man (1:13)
The Lamb (5:6)
The Shepherd (7:17)
The Word of God (19:13)

The distinguished teacher, who amazed teachers, has entered the history of the universe, as He has divided history to what is called B.C. (Before Christ), and A.D. *anno domini* or (After Christ). He has opened the door of eternity to all people, and has welcomed all nations to believe on Him. The door is still open and the *anno domini* is still running until He comes again!

Chapter 3

The Message of the Master

"When Jesus had finished saying these things, the crowds were amazed at his teaching, because he taught as one who has authority and not as their teachers of the law" (Mt 7:28).

What did Jesus teach?

Jesus taught a divine message. He gave an elaborate definition for any subject He handled and confirmed the biblical references that were related to the topic. Donald Guthrie[11] pointed out that the message for Jesus was more important than the method of His teaching. In other words, the method was a means to an end. He also added that Jesus' teaching centered on the Father, the Son, the Holy Spirit, man and fellowship. The Master used the past tense as a point of reference only; but the two main domains in which He gave His message were the present and the future.

Jesus came to earth on a mission; to show people what God was really like. Anyone who has seen Him (Jesus) "has seen the Father" (Jn 14:9*b*). Edward Kuhlman[12] wrote:

> Having submitted to the mastery of God the Father, he came not to do his own will, but the will of God, who sent him (John 5:30). He excited the crowd's attention and earned his disciples' admiration by the personal mastery that controlled and emanated from him. It hallmarked his ministry. Unlike the Scribes and Pharisees, he did not reduce his teaching to an insipid cookbook approach or cloud it with undecipherable esoteric jargon. He spoke with accuracy and authority.

When Jesus came in person, we saw a humble, gentle and kind-hearted God, who took the shape of a servant. We saw the real person: forgiving and benevolent. In the Old Testament, the Father was the *God of Law*. Through Jesus Christ, we have the *God of Grace*. If we, as humans, with our shortcomings, have forgotten what God had done with His people when He led them out of the land of Egypt to the Promised Land, we cannot possibly forget the crucifixion scene, when Jesus was crucified with two robbers. To realize what He did for each one of us is overwhelming. Through the Law, man had to work very hard according to its provisions, to gain reward based on one's performance. Those who had followed the Law could hardly change, and therefore, there was dire need for grace, as the Scripture says, "For all have sinned and fall short of the glory of God, and are justified freely by his grace through the redemption that came by Christ Jesus" (Rom 3:23-24). In order to live in the grace of God, each individual has to express interest and need for it. One also has to accept God's grace in sending us the Holy Spirit, which leads and empowers us. It is the gift of God. Warren Benson[13] wrote in that respect:

> In teaching, Jesus Christ was always building into people's lives principles that will endure and transcend the existential moment. Those who walked with him became a community of learners.

Jesus serves as a model teacher that can guide and comfort us in various life situations and brightens our lives. The 'Sermon on the Mount' is a great source of the Master's teaching upon which most of the Christian doctrines are built. The sermon was initially meant to be introduced to the disciples, but it looks like the multitudes were listeners of what came to be the highlight of Jesus' teaching. Warren Benson[14] wrote:

> Jesus Christ had a complete grasp of the subject; his skill in teaching had no limits. Even his enemies admitted that he taught with power and authority. His followers respected

Jesus because in time they understood that he had come from the Father as the Incarnate Son.

Jesus summed up His message in the two most important of all the commandments: Love God and love your neighbor (Mt 22:34-40). To love God and your neighbor means you have to go back to the creation order, to keep a relationship with God and with others. Man had sinned and this love for God and neighbor did not play out well. Therefore, God sent His only begotten Son to redeem the sinners. Through the redemption process, Jesus Christ reconciled us with the Father against whom we had sinned, and the wages of our sin would have taken us to inevitable death. This reconciliation brings us back to love God and to love our neighbor. Without this positive relationship with God and with others, we will be unable to grow. And in order to have a relationship with God we must know who God is and what the kingdom of heaven looks like. One of the twelve disciples had a specific request from Jesus:

> Philip said, 'Lord, show us the Father, and that will be enough for us'. Jesus answered, 'Don't you know me, Philip, even after I have been among you such a long time? Anyone who has seen me has seen the Father' (Jn 14:8-9*a*).

The Master Teacher's message included doctrines for a true Christian. Those doctrines were introduced in the form of discourses, sermons, criticisms, conversations, arguments, rebukes, acts of healing and raising from the dead, as well as many other forms and deeds. The main theme of Jesus' teaching was, "Repent for the kingdom of God is near" (Mt 4:17b).

1. Jesus' Message to the Tempter (Mt 4)

In order to begin His teaching on solid ground, Jesus started by defeating the tempter, the devil. The format of teaching that Jesus used with the devil started with challenge and rebuke and ended with the Master's victory. The devil tested Jesus three times.

- a. The tempter came to Jesus and said, "If you are the Son of God, tell these stones to become bread." Jesus answered, "It is written: Man does not live on bread alone, but on every word that comes from the mouth of God" (Mt 4:3b-4).

- b. The second test took place when the tempter took Jesus to the highest point of the temple in Jerusalem, "If you are the Son of God", he said, "throw yourself down. For it is written: 'He will command his angels concerning you and they will lift you up in their hands, so that you will not strike your foot against a stone.'"

  Jesus answered him, "Do not put the Lord your God to the test" (Mt 4:6-7).

- c. The third lesson that Jesus taught the devil took place at the top of a high mountain. Satan showed Him the kingdoms of the world and their splendor and said, "All this I will give you if you bow down and worship me." Jesus rebuked the tempter saying, "Away from me, Satan! For it is written: 'Worship the Lord your God and serve him only'" (Mt 4:9-10).

The Scripture states that after those three temptations, the devil left on his own, as he was defeated. The angels ascended from heaven and attended Jesus. Having overcome the tempter, Jesus began teaching the people who had long expected Him. Warren Benson[15] stated, "He [Jesus] did not major in methods of teaching but rather in ministry with people."

2. Teaching through Healing (Mt 8:14-17)

Jesus' compassionate love to humankind was manifest in His healing of the diseased and the afflicted, relieving them from their infirmities and severe pain. Some were demon-possessed. Yet, He made sure that every person that He healed would proclaim His message and live in Him. Many people were attracted to Him to hear His message as well as to witness the miracles of healing.

3. Beatitudes (Mt 5:3-12)

Jesus started the 'Sermon on the Mount' with the positive note, using the well-known beatitudes. He said:

Blessed are:

...the poor in spirit→theirs is the kingdom of God.

...the mourners→ they will be comforted.

...the meek→they will inherit the earth.

...those who hunger and thirst for righteousness→they will be filled.

...the merciful→they will be shown mercy.

...the pure in heart→they will see God.

...the peacemakers→they will be called the sons of God.

...the persecuted because of righteousness→theirs is the kingdom of heaven.

...you, when people insult you, persecute you and falsely say all kinds of false things about you because of me [Jesus]→you will be rewarded in heaven.

4. Woes (Lk 6:24-26)

Jesus also warned against the wages of sin by use of woes.

Woe to you who:

...are rich→you have already received your comfort.

...are well fed now→you will go hungry.

... laugh now→you will mourn and weep.

... all men speak well of you→that is how their fathers treated the false prophets.

5. Teaching on Knowing Oneself (Mt 5:13-16)

The Master Teacher teaches us that if we do His will, we are like the salt of the earth. Yet if the salt goes bad or loses its saltiness, it is just useless and should be thrown away and trampled by people. Jesus also likens the good Christians to the light of the world that cannot be hidden, like a city on a hill. He wants us to make ourselves visible-to let the light shine out through our good deeds and guide others to God's word, which will result in saving lives.

6. Teaching of the Law and Teaching of the Master (Mt 5:17-37)

The teaching of Jesus was always compared to the teaching of the Law. Jesus clarified that issue in His teaching by stating that He did not come to abolish or contradict the Law and the prophecies; He came to complete and to fulfill them. In that respect, Jesus openly attacked the teachings of the Pharisees and the rabbis. He said:

> For I tell you that unless your righteousness surpasses that of the Pharisees and the teachers of the law, you will certainly not enter the kingdom of heaven (Mt 5:20).

Jesus also taught on murder, adultery, divorce and oath fulfillment. He gave us insights on how God judges sin comparing earthly judgment with God's judgment.

a. *On the Crime of Murder*: Any murderer is liable to the judgment of the Law, which most likely results in death. Jesus goes further to enlighten us on the sanctity of a Christian person by saying that if someone says angrily to another person, 'Raca', which is an Aramaic expression of contempt meaning 'You fool', he or she should be sentenced by the Supreme Sanhedrin (Court). Furthermore, if someone insults a brother, saying, 'fool', he or she deserves hell. The Master's advice is to settle our disputes with an adversary, lest we should be judged in court, spend all our money, and may end up in prison. Jesus also teaches us about God's judgment at the end of times (Mt 5:21-26).

b. *On the Sin of Adultery*: The Law commands us not to commit adultery. Jesus adds that if a man looks at a woman lustfully, he has already committed the sin of adultery with her, in his own heart (Mt 5:27-30).

c. *On the Issue of Divorce:* The Law constitutes that anyone who divorces his wife has to give her a certificate of divorce. Jesus taught us that anyone who divorces his wife for a reason other than adultery, causes her to commit adultery, and any man who marries a divorced woman commits adultery (Mt 5:31-32).

d. *On Oath Fulfillment:* The Law constitutes that no one should break an oath with God. Jesus adds that we should not swear at all, but simply say 'yes' or 'no' and anything more than that comes from the evil one (Mt 5:33-37).

7. Lessons on True Love (Mt 5:43-48; Mk 12:29)

The Master Teacher, the Savior, the Lord of love and mercy, offers the most effective fruits of true Christian love. Love of others constitutes making treasures in heaven in such acts as forgiveness, love of enemies, helping the needy, praying and fasting. The doctrines of the Master stand out as the distinguished fruits of love that make the Christian faith distinct from any other faith.

- a. *Forgiveness:* On the premise of 'eye for eye and tooth for tooth', Jesus teaches us not to retaliate against an evil person. Furthermore, the Master gives the distinguished unparalleled behavior in tolerance and forgiveness, "If someone strikes you on the right cheek, turn to him the other also. And if someone wants to sue you and take your tunic, let him have your cloak as well" (Mt 5:39*b*-40).
- b. *Love of Enemies*: The Master's teaching on who to love and how to love are the most defining bases of Christianity. The verse that says, "Love your enemies" stands out as a clear distinction between Christianity and all other faiths (Mt 5:44; Lk 6:27, 35). Jesus is very explicit about loving enemies and He offers several situations to illustrate His view of love. He also said, "If you love those who love you,

what reward would you get? Are not even the tax-collectors doing that?" (Mt 5:46).

We can really be called the 'sons of God', if we love our enemies (Mt 5:43-48; Lk 6:32-36). Another demonstration of love is to do good for those who hate us, to bless those who curse us. If someone asks us for help or material, we should give that person what he/she asks for and not demand back what we had given.

c. *Giving to the Needy*: Jesus directs us to give to the needy. Yet, we should be careful not to disclose what we give to other people. Otherwise, we lose our reward from God. Our assistance will be done in private, whereas our reward from God will be made public (Mt 6:1-4). Jesus also remarkably said, "Give to the one who asks you, and do not turn away from the one who wants to borrow from you" (Mt 5:42). In this regard, the Master cautions us:

> Do not give dogs what is sacred; do not throw your pearls to pigs. If you do, they may trample them under their feet, and then turn and tear you to pieces (Mt 7:6).

d. *Praying: Ask-Seek-Knock:*
How do we pray? The 'Lord's Prayer' is a model to follow (Mt 6:9-13).

What does the Lord's Prayer consist of?

"Our Father in heaven: *addressing the Father*

Hallowed be your name: *glorifying God's holiness*

Your kingdom come: *acknowledging God's sovereignty*

Your will be done on earth: *submitting to God's will*

As it is in heaven: *acknowledging God's authority*

Give us today our daily bread: *requesting daily needs*

Forgive us our debts: *asking for God's forgiveness*

As we also have forgiven our debtors: *declaring our love and forgiveness to others*

Lead us not into temptation: *pleading for protection*

But deliver us from the evil one: *requesting deliverance*

For yours is the kingdom: *honoring God's authority*

The power and the glory: *glorifying God's supremacy*

For ever." *acknowledging God's eternity.*

Jesus reminds us that hypocrites like to stand in synagogues (assemblies) and at the corners of the streets when they pray, to be praised by men (Mt 6:5-8; 7:7-12). Jesus advises us:
- to go to our own room [a private place], close our door and pray to the unseen God, who sees in secret and will reward us,
- not to repeat the words in vain (even pagans do that). Our Father knows our needs, even before we mention them,
- not to be redundant, and,
- to ask and we shall be given.

Why do we pray?

We pray to keep the channel constantly connected between God and ourselves. It should be a non-stop relationship. The Arabic word for prayer is *'salah'* from the root *'wasala'* meaning 'to connect'.

How often should we pray?

Jesus did not give us a specific number of prayers. He told His disciples that they should pray *always* (Lk 18:1). In the parable about the 'Widow and the Judge', Jesus said clearly:

> Will not God bring about justice for his chosen ones, who cry out [pray] to him day and night? Will he keep putting them off? (Lk 18:7).

c. *Fasting*: It is a process that accompanies prayer. Jesus fasted for forty days and nights prior to His initial ministry of the kingdom of God. Fasting should not be done beyond our physical ability. Nevertheless, it is the best way of submitting our prayers to God. Fasting and praying work miracles in our lives (Mt 6:16-18).

8. Lessons on a Better Life:

The Master Teacher highlighted for us ways for a peaceful life on earth. He likened a true believer to a 'wise person' who is identified as one who hears Jesus' words and puts them in practice. He or she resembles a man who built his house on the solid rock that cannot be easily destroyed by rain or storm. Likewise, a solid Christian rests his faith on God, and is not affected by the negative environment where he lives. (Mt 7:24-27). Jesus started this teaching session by the introductory note (warm-up) that most successful teachers do today. He spoke about 'The Narrow and Wide Gates', pointing out that the gate to destruction (hell) is wide and broad, through which many will enter. The gate to heaven is narrow and full of hardships; yet, it is the only way that leads to eternal life. Few will enter through it. Nevertheless, Jesus is standing at the door of your heart, if you open your heart to Him, He will come in. (Mt 7:13-14).

The Master went on to explain specific situations in life:

a. *Do Not Worry*: Jesus said, "No one can serve two masters" (Mt 6:24*a*). By that, He meant 'God and money'. If you really have faith in God, you will not worry about getting money to satisfy your needs of food, drink and clothing. By following this advice, many of the problems of the world would be solved. One of the great attractions in the Master's teaching is His use of the surrounding nature to illustrate His point. He used the birds in the sky and the lilies in the field: those birds do not worry, yet, God feeds them. Jesus also referred to the lilies that are more magnificent in the way they are dressed than Solomon in all his glory (Mt 6:25-34*a*). At the end of this description, Jesus connected the introductory note with the concluding teaching point when He said, "For the pagans run after all these things, and your heavenly Father knows that you need them. But seek first his kingdom and his righteousness, and all these things will be given to you as well" (Mt 6:32-33).

b. *Do Not Judge Others:* Jesus teaches us not to condemn others because we are all born with sin. He said, "Do not judge or you too will be judged. For in the same way you judge others, you will be judged, and with the measure you use, it will be measured to you" (Mt 7:1-2).

Jesus also made a great simile by saying:

> Why do you look the speck of sawdust in your brother's eye and pay no attention to the plank in your own eye? How can you say to your brother, 'Let me take the speck out of your eye' when all the time there is a plank in your own eye? You hypocrite, first take the plank out of your own eye, and then you will see clearly to remove the speck from your brother's eye (Mt 7:3-5; Lk 6:37-38).

c. *Beware of False Prophets:* The existence of false prophets was, and remains, a very controversial aspect that was predominant at the time of Jesus, and later on. Jesus projected that false prophets would claim that they would be sent by God. Jesus was clear: No prophet would come after Him. (Mt 7:15-20).

A True Believer

The Gospel of John introduces a true receiver of the message of the Master Teacher. As a true witness of Jesus, Nicodemus demonstrated, through word and deed, his full trust in Jesus, and in seeking the truth about the 'kingdom of God'. He was mentioned three times, only in the Gospel of John (Jn 3:1-21; 7:50-52; 19:38-42).

Nicodemus was a Pharisee and a member of the Jewish ruling council. Jesus taught Nicodemus in an impressive one-on-one session. The first mention of Nicodemus was when he went alone at night to meet Jesus. He came to Jesus at night, possibly for three reasons. First, he was afraid of his fellow religious leaders. Secondly, he needed to have a private time with Jesus when no one was around, as he had specific questions to ask the Lord. Thirdly, he witnessed Jesus' miracles and was sure that He came from God. Yet, he wanted some personal assurance that he, Nicodemus, would inherit the kingdom of God.

Jesus gave Nicodemus the attention that He would have given to a multitude. It is noteworthy that Jesus addressed the most memorized verse in the Bible to Nicodemus (Jn 3:16).

Although Jesus was sometimes reluctant to speak to the Pharisees because He knew their unbelieving hearts, Nicodemus was a serious seeker for the truth, and had the innocent simple mind of a child.

Nicodemus demonstrated the appropriate honor and respect to the Master by saying:

> Rabbi, we know you are a teacher who has come from God. For no one could perform the miraculous signs you are doing if God were not with him (Jn 3:2*b*).

Jesus explained to him that the re-birth from God was the only way to inherit the kingdom of God. The Gospel does not mention much about Nicodemus' rebirth, but his actions that followed, explicitly demonstrated that he was born again.

The second mention of Nicodemus took place when the Jewish leaders sent the temple guards to arrest Jesus. They came back without Him and the leaders rebuked them. Nicodemus could not be silent. The Scripture says:

> Nicodemus, who had gone to Jesus earlier and who was of their number, asked, 'Does our law condemn a man without first hearing him to find out what he is doing?' They replied, 'Are you from Galilee, too? Look into it, and you will find that a prophet does not come out of Galilee' (Jn 7:50-52).

The third mention of Nicodemus was when Jesus died on the cross. Joseph of Arimathea and Nicodemus went to Pilate to request the body of Jesus for burial. The Scripture documents, "He [Joseph] was accompanied by Nicodemus, the man who earlier had visited Jesus at night. Nicodemus brought a mixture of myrrh and aloes, about seventy-five pounds. Taking Jesus' body, the two of them wrapped it, with the spices, in strips of linen…" (Jn 19:39-40*a*).

The first time Nicodemus went to see Jesus; he went alone and at night, secretly. He was afraid. Yet, that fear changed into a courageous and daring witness who confronted the Jewish leaders and the Roman governor Pilate, who condemned Jesus and sent Him to crucifixion. Nicodemus volunteered to sacrifice his prestigious position as a leader, counselor and teacher in the Jewish council because his Lord and Master was his priority. He would rather lose his position than lose his eternity. Moreover, Nicodemus demonstrated courage, love and devotion by accompanying another most loving disciple of Jesus, Joseph of Arimathea, to request the body of Jesus for burial.

Chapter 4

The Master's Teaching Methods

"No one can come to me unless the Father who sent me draws him, and I will raise him up at the last day. It is written in the prophets: 'They will all be taught by God'. Everyone who listens to the Father and learns from him comes to me" (Jn 6:44b-45).

In the gospels, the terms 'teacher' and the Aramaic title 'rabbi' were used frequently to address or refer to Jesus. Moreover, Jesus used this title for self-designation. (Mt 10:2-5, 23:8).

How did the Master teach?

Although He had no formal education, the Master Teacher taught using the most effective methods. His teaching methods surpassed the most advanced methods in teaching. He taught using different formats, styles and devices. Robert Stein[16] wrote, "The

The Teaching of the Master

gospels indicate that Jesus was an extraordinary teacher." Stephen Arterburn[17] describes how Jesus operated differently from other teachers in one of his book introduction:

> ......the way Jesus did things on this earth was so different from how many of us operate. Often we act in ways to make us feel good about ourselves or to support a tradition we've adopted or to uphold some cherished rule. But Jesus always valued relationships over rules. Whether it was healing a person on the Sabbath or sharing a meal with a known "sinner", Jesus acted in unpredictable, unexpected, and life-changing ways. And the fact is, wherever the Master traveled and ministered, two things inevitably happened: People's lives were changed and the established religious order was upset.

Jesus does not expect any learner to be superior to Him, but to be like Him, and to learn from Him. In reference to Jesus' statement on the teacher and learner, documented in Mt 10:24-25, Lee Magness[18] pointed out:

> One statement of Jesus, almost an understatement, may provide the clearest insight into the purposeful way Jesus taught and the objectives he had in mind, 'a learner is not superior to the teacher, nor is a slave superior to his master. It is

sufficient for the learner to become like the teacher, and the slave like his master.'

The methods of Jesus, as well as the content of His teaching, were a magnet that drew thousands to Him. His message could mesmerize the audience to the extent that they forgot some of their basic needs, such as food. The miracle of feeding the five thousand with five loaves and two fish is a good example (Jn 6:5-15). People were attracted to the Master Teacher for many reasons, among them:

a. The message was important to them. Jesus' main message was: 'The kingdom of God has come'. The voice of prophecy was being heard once again, after four hundred years of no prophecy. The Jews had waited for the voice of God through prophecy, and had longed for the fulfillment of that prophecy about the Messiah who, according to their rabbis, would deliver them from the foreign invasion of the Roman Empire.

b. The personality of the Master Teacher was extraordinary. His teaching was divine. He spoke with authority and doctrine, not like the teachers of the Law (Mt 7:28-29; Mk 1:22).

c. The methods with which He taught were new. The Master Teacher used a variety of literary forms and poetic devices to convey His message. The forms Jesus used included 'Discourse' such as the 'Sermon on the Mount' (Mt 5-7), the 'Charging of the Twelve' (Mt 10) and 'Discourse on Relationships' (Mt 5:27-48). Secondly, His message included the 'Parable', such as the parable of 'The Lost Sheep' (Lk 15:3-7). He also used 'Conversation' as a method, such as His conversation with the Samaritan woman (Jn 4:1-26). In His teaching, Jesus also taught through 'Question and Answer', such as when the disciples of John the Baptist asked Him about fasting (Mt 9:14-17). Moreover, the Master used 'Prediction' to convey His message, like when He predicted that Peter would deny Him (Jn 13:38). One of the most effective methods of Jesus was to teach through 'Prayer'. Jesus prayed for Himself, for His disciples and for the whole world, including His enemies (Mt 5:44; Lk 6:28). Jesus also taught through 'Miracle' such as the 'Healing of the Ten Lepers' (Lk 17:11-19). The Master also used the format of the 'Beatitude' (Mt 5:3-12) and the 'Woe' (Lk 6:24-26). Sometimes, He used the format of 'Argument' to teach a point or to convince His audience of the truth of His message. He said:

> Do not believe me, unless I do what my Father does. But if I do it, even though you do not believe me, believe the miracles, that you may learn and understand that the Father is in me, and I in the Father (Jn 10:31-38).

Before Jesus charged the twelve disciples to spread the gospel to people, He trained them on a daily basis. Lawrence Richards[19] commented on Jesus' discipling:

Jesus maintained an intimate teaching ministry with his disciples. He answered their questions about the day's events and questioned them in turn. The disciples observed Jesus' life while traveling with him and Jesus gave them life assignments, as when he sent them out two by two. This powerful intimate form of instruction is best understood as discipling.

The parable is one of the most distinctive features of Jesus' teaching ministry. We have in the gospels from thirty-seven up to seventy parables, depending on if we consider some of the sayings as parables. It was an extremely useful method because Jesus used it to introduce the center of His teaching on the arrival of the kingdom of God. This new intimacy with God would enable His followers to live the ethics of the kingdom. Secondly, through His exquisite use of parables, Jesus also avoided controversy that would erupt by the Roman authorities. Sometimes, the disciples could not understand the allegorical references to which the parable referred. Therefore, Jesus explained the parables in private to the believers; those who were prepared to accept the message. Moreover, Jesus used allegorical references in the parables to teach a certain message while avoiding the antagonistic attitude of some of the listeners such as the Pharisees. Thirdly, a parable was extremely effective because the scenes and the characters were taken from real life situations, such as the parable of the 'Lost Coin' (Lk 15:8-10), and the parable of the 'Dishonest

Manager' (Lk 16:1-13). In His teaching, the Master made use of real environmental surroundings when He said, "Consider the ravens, for they neither sow nor reap..." (Lk 12:24), or "If you have faith as small as a mustard seed you can say to this mountain 'Move from here to there', and it will move. Nothing will be impossible for you" (Mt 17:20b-21). A fourth reason that made the use of parables so effective is that Jesus used them to introduce deep theological concepts that could be difficult for the listeners to understand if He used abstract ideas. The Master Teacher used simple life experiences to illustrate the deepest spiritual mysteries of the kingdom of heaven. Warren Benson[20] wrote in that regard:

> Christ never lost touch with those he was teaching, despite the loftiness of his content or the holiness of his character. He knew how to adapt to their level of understanding and used the familiar to explain the profound.

Jesus also used other literary formats such as 'Beatitude' and 'Woe'.

'Beatitude' is an expression of blessedness or thankfulness for a certain positive ethic or Christian virtue. Beatitudes existed in the Old Testament (Ps 2:12b, 32:1-2; Prov 8:34) and in the New Testament (Mt 5:3-11; Lk 6:20-22; Rom 4:7-8; Rev 1:3). The beatitude starts with a clause stating the blessing, followed by the reason, as well as the result of the blessing in the second clause. Beatitudes are key reminders of radical Christian detachment from the world. The blessed are those who live by certain spiritual values that may seem to the world as weaknesses, but in God's eye they act as 'interim ethic', that binds only for the short period on earth, before the everlasting life that would start by Jesus' second coming. The 'Sermon on the Mount', started with 'Beatitudes' such as, "Blessed are the meek for they will inherit the earth" (Mt 5:5).

'Woe' addresses the second person 'you'. Luke's four beatitudes are followed by four corresponding woes that make the picture perfect in the mind of any listener (Lk 6:24-26). They represent the sharp contrast of those who are not blessed when God's kingdom comes to judge the world. Jesus said:

> Woe to you Pharisees, because you love the most important seats in the synagogues and greetings in the marketplaces. Woe to you because you are like unmarked graves, which men walk over without knowing it (Lk 11:43-44).

The literary and poetic devices and styles that Jesus used were numerous (Italics are used for clarification):

Antithetical Parallelism: In order to tell us to love our enemies Jesus said:

> *Love* your *enemies, do good* to those who *hate* you, *bless* those who *curse* you (Lk 6:27*b*-28*a*).

Metaphor: In order to tell us: 'Do not worry', Jesus said:

> Consider how the *lilies* grow. They *do not labor* or *spin*. Yet I tell you, *not even Solomon* in all his splendor was *dressed like one of these* (Lk 12:27).

Riddle: Referring to His death and resurrection, Jesus said to the Pharisees:

> Destroy this temple and I will raise it again in three days (Jn 2:19*b*).

Pun: On growth and keeping the faith, Jesus said:

> *I am* the *true vine* and my *Father* is the *gardener* (Jn 15:1).

Synonym: On the importance of prayer, the Master said:

> *Ask* and it will be *given* to you; *seek* and you shall *find*; *knock* and the door will be *opened to* you (Mt 7:7).

Hyperbole: Jesus wanted to make it clear that a man cannot worship God and money. He said:

> It is easier for a *camel to go through the eye of a needle*, than for a *rich man to enter the kingdom of God* (Mk10:25).

Simile: Jesus had sent seventy-two people to spread the gospel. The Scripture says:

> The seventy-two returned with joy and said, 'Lord, even demons submit to us in your name'. He replied, 'I saw *Satan fall like lightning from heaven'* (Lk 10:17-18).

Paradox: The Master used this style to introduce a statement that may seem contradictory, but it expresses a certain truth. He said:

> If you have *faith as small as a mustard seed,* you can say to this *mountain* 'move from here to there' and it will *move.* (Mt 17:20*b*-21*a*).

Counter-question: The soldiers came to arrest Jesus. The Scripture registers Jesus' counter-question:

> *Am I leading a rebellion"*, said Jesus, "that you have come out with swords and clubs to capture me? *Every day I was*

with you teaching in the temple courts, and you did not arrest me (Mk 14:48-49*a*).

Proverb: Jesus used proverbs from the Old Testament in such as quoting from Hosea 6:6*a* when God was addressing the unrepentant Israel:

> But go and learn what this means: 'I desire *mercy, not sacrifice*' (Mt 9:13*a*).

Chiastic Parallelism: From Jesus' parable of the 'Prodigal Son' the father said to the older son:

> …But we had to celebrate and be glad, because this brother of yours was *dead* and is *alive* again, he was l*ost* and is *found* (Lk 15:32).

Synonymous Parallels: From the 'Sermon on the Mount', Jesus said:

> If someone *strikes* you on the *right* cheek, *turn to* him *the other* also. And if someone wants to sue you and *take* your tunic, *let him have* your cloak as well. If someone forces you *to go one* mile, *go* with him *two* miles. *Give* to the one who *asks* you… (Mt 5:39b-42a).

Repetition: Jesus used this effective method in teaching to emphasize ideas, statements and doctrines. In the Gospel of John 6:50-51, notice Jesus' repetition in His use of *living bread* and derivatives and synonyms such as *life, not die,* and *live* to illustrate His idea about 'life in Him'. He said:

> But here is the *bread* that comes down from heaven, which a man may eat and *not die.* I am the *living bread* that came down from heaven. If a man eats of this *bread,* he will *live* forever. This *bread* is my flesh, which I will give for the *life* of the world (Jn 6:50-51).

Bread is repeated four times. Live/living/not die/life also appear four times.

Jesus used repetition primarily to highlight a point, as well as to proceed to the next point. After stating the crucial fact about the believers' 'life in Him', Jesus proceeded to the target point about 'eternal life'. He said:

> Our forefathers ate manna and *died*, but he who feeds on this bread will *live forever* (Jn 6:58*b*).

Jesus' teaching is transformational because it is the process of spiritual change. Nevertheless, Jesus first looked for a person's physical need and worked on satisfying that need, before He proceeded to transform a person's life forever. It is the process of healing the body and the soul. The Samaritan woman was in need of water, so He offered her the living water (Jn 4:1-42). He fed the five thousand who came to hear Him and offered to them the message of eternal life (Jn 6:5-13). Whatever method or device He used, His ultimate goal was to proclaim the kingdom of God. In John 9, we follow the story of the blind man that Jesus healed. The blind man started the scene as a beggar who was born blind. The Scriptures say that Jesus saw him and *proceeded* to help him. Jesus knows our limitations and He volunteers to fill the gap. Most likely, the blind man listened to the conversation between the Master and the disciples discussing whose sin caused that man's blindness, whether it was his or his parents. Wanting to heal him, Jesus spat on the dirt and made a mud that He put on the man's eyes, and asked him to go and wash in the pool of Siloam. When the man could then see and went to his house, his neighbors saw the physical transformation and started to debate among themselves. He boldly addressed his neighbors who suspected that he was the blind man they knew saying, "I am *the* man!" (Jn 9:9*b*). The blind man turned into a preacher. The physical transformation that took place in this man's eyesight, did not only transform his vision, but it also transformed his spirit. In contrast to his silence and status of a beggar that would certainly be associated with humility and a low-key attitude, he became a spokesperson, a strong witness for Jesus. The poor beggar became a strong defender whose famous line echoed in the neighborhood when he said, "He is a prophet" (Jn 9:17*b*). The verses in John 9:24-41 illustrate that transformation.

Secondly, we find that the transformation that takes place because of Jesus' teaching is also a process of correcting many of the false concepts among the people. The Jews had carried the commandment on remembering the Sabbath to an extreme (Ex 20:8-9). They openly criticized Jesus when He healed on the Sabbath and were angry when the disciples plucked corn from the fields and ate them on the Sabbath (Mt 12:1-8). Jesus reminded the Pharisees of what David had done when he and his companions were hungry and entered the house of God, and ate the consecrated bread. Jesus said:

> If you had known what these words mean 'I desire mercy, not sacrifice', you would have not condemned the innocent. For the Son of Man is the Lord of the Sabbath (Mt 12:7-8).

The Pharisees also followed the traditions that the rabbis had made, and ignored God's commandments. They drifted from the truth. A clear example took place when they came to Jesus complaining that His disciples had not washed their hands before eating. Jesus pinpointed the fact that God's commandments are the source of our doctrine, not the traditions of men. He reminded them of the commandment that they had to honor their father and mother; otherwise, they deserved death. Yet they considered that a gift to a parent was a gift to God. He said to them:

You hypocrites! Isaiah was right when he prophesied about you 'These people honor me with their lips but their hearts are far from me' (Isa 29:13; Mt 15:1-11: 8).

Thirdly, through His teaching, the Master Teacher corrected many of the concepts on social relations such as marriage and divorce, helping the poor, praying and fasting, and honoring parents. Jesus used the Old Testament quotes, yet He added more authority, being the divine teacher, the Son of God. He used familiar expressions and quotes from the Old Testament to clarify an idea on a relationship. Nevertheless, under the new life, Jesus fulfilled the Law and made it more meaningful and more applicable. He said that He came to throw a sword not peace. So instead of saying 'honor your parents so your days will be prolonged', He would tell us to honor our parents, otherwise we would die. Some verses illustrate the aspect of honoring parents.

In the Old Testament:

> If a man curses his father or mother, his lamp will be snuffed out in pitch darkness (Prov 20:20).

and

> Honor your father and your mother as the Lord your God has commanded you; so that you may live long, and that it may go well with you in the land the Lord God is giving you (Deut 5:16).

In the New Testament, Jesus said:

> For God said 'Honor your father and mother' and 'Anyone who curses his father or mother must be put to death' (Mt 15:4).

On the issue of justice, Jesus referred to what Solomon said, "To do what is right and just is more acceptable to the Lord than sacrifice" (Prov 21:3). Yet in contrast, Jesus said:

> But go and learn what this means: 'I desire mercy not sacrifice.' For I have not come to call the righteous, but sinners (Mt 9:13).

Part II

Effectiveness of the Master's Teaching

Chapter 5

Permanent Change

"I am the true vine and my Father is the gardener. He cuts off every branch in me that bears no fruit, while every branch that does bear fruit he trims clean so that it will be even more fruitful. You are already clean because of the word I have spoken to you" (Jn 15:1-3).

What a good feeling Christians have when they become parts of the body of Christ! Jesus likens Himself to the 'True Vine' and His Father is the 'Gardener'. Christians are the 'branches' of that true vine. They are nurtured from the food that the vine provides. They have become clean as they feed from the pure living water of God's word. They can become active and productive.

The discourse of the 'True Vine' is a message of love and comfort, of encouragement and assurance. It was shortly before the Last

Supper, and before Jesus was betrayed and delivered to be later tortured and crucified (Jn 15:1-17).

It is generally agreed that Jesus' discourse of the 'True Vine' took place after the charge of the Scribes to the disciples that they ate with 'unclean' hands (Mt 15:1-20; Mk 7:1-23). The Gospel of Mark documents a ceremonial tradition of the elders concerning washing of the hands (Mk 7:1-8). Alfred Edersheim[21] made a lengthy argument on the issue of cleanliness. He mentioned the two great rival teachers and heroes Hillel and Shammai who had headed the two schools of Jewish traditionalism, prior to Jesus' teaching. They had many differences in their interpretation of the Law, yet they had agreed on eighteen issues, among which was the issue on defilement. The decree of washing of the hands before eating was among the issues upon which they agreed. Immediately before Christ started His divine teaching, the decree on the washing of the hands (*Netilath Yadayim*) was approved by the rabbinic ordinance. Edersheim wrote:

> This fully accounts for the zeal which the Scribes displayed and explains the extreme minuteness of details with which Saint Mark calls attention to the Pharisaic practice.......Thus it will be seen, that the language employed by the Evangelist affords most valuable indirect confirmation of trustworthiness of his gospel, as not only showing intimate familiarity

with the minutiae of Jewish tradition, but giving prominence to what was then a present controversy.

Hillel and Shammai connected themselves with those eighteen decrees intended to separate the Jews from all contact with the Gentiles. Even the touch of a Gentile's clothes might involve such defilement that on coming from the market any Jew should immerse to purify and clean oneself. The concern here is Jesus' attitude towards those ordinances of purification. When He replied to the charge of the Scribes against His disciples, He neither vindicated their conduct, nor apologized for breaking the rabbinic ordinance. Jesus chose not to mention those ordinances, as they did not reflect the Scriptures. The charge of the Scribes implied that the Pharisees revered ordinances of men more than they revered the Holy Scripture. Yet Jesus firmly stated that the word of God was above tradition, which was utterly incompatible with the Scripture. He revealed the hypocrisy of their system of traditionalism in focusing on unimportant irrelevant issues and ignoring the most vital of God's commandments. The Master Teacher quoted from Isaiah:

> These people honor me with their lips, but their hearts are far from me. They worship me in vain; their teachings are but rules taught by men (Mk 7:6*b*-7; Mt 15:8; Isa 29:13).

Jesus openly opposed tradition and enunciated the fundamental principal of His own interpretation of the Law. The Law was moral and addressed man as a moral being-having heart and conscience. The Master emphasized that nothing that enters the body defiles the body but what comes out of the mouth is an expression of the heart, whether positive or negative. The ordinance is contradictory to what the moral Law emphasized.

The whole discourse, documented in the seventh chapter of the Gospel of Mark, took place while the multitude stood aside, not interfering in the discussion. Yet, as soon as the Scribes left, Jesus called the multitude to Him and said:

> Listen to me everyone, and understand this. Nothing outside a man can make him 'unclean' by going into him. Rather, it is what comes out of a man that makes him 'unclean' (Mk 7:14*b*-16).

In the passage on the vine, Jesus calls Christians 'friends' because they are given all the truth about the kingdom of God (Jn 15:3). They are no longer called 'servants' because a servant does not know what his master does. A permanent change has taken place. Matthew Henry[22] wrote about the discourse of 'The True Vine' in his commentary:

> We must be fruitful. From a vine we look for grapes (Isa 5:2) and from a Christian we look for Christianity, this is the fruit; a Christian temper and disposition, a Christian life and conversation, Christian devotion and Christian designs. We must honor God, and do good, and exemplify the purity and power of the religion we profess, and this is bearing fruit.

In His discourse on the vine, and before Jesus was led to be crucified, buried and resurrected, three points are noteworthy. First, He wanted to make sure that His disciples, having received the faith; would continue to live in Him. Secondly, He wanted to underscore that they would stay close to each other and love one another. Thirdly, He wanted to confirm that they would remain fruitful.

In the fourteenth chapter of the Gospel of John, Jesus had promised the Holy Spirit:

> If you love me, you will obey what I command. And I will ask the Father, and he will give you another Counselor, to be with you forever - the Spirit of truth (Jn 14:15-17a).

This discourse is extremely important as it explains the relationship between the Father and the Son, between the Father and the church, and between Christ and the church; a relationship that results in permanent change.

The Father, or the 'Gardener', cuts off every branch that does not bear fruit. This refers to the unfruitful person in God's field; the person who does not nourish from God's word, whether by refusing the message or by mere indifference to God's work in one's life. On the other hand, every branch that does bear fruit, God trims clean, so that it will be even more fruitful. God loves us so much that He keeps working on our deficiencies and shortcomings because we are extremely precious to Him. Jesus also assures that God's glory is manifested when Christians spread the news of the gospel and bring others to the Christian faith. Christians should show themselves to be disciples of Jesus. Most importantly, as the Father loves the Son, the Son loves the church.

Jesus or, the 'True Vine' announces to His disciples that a change has taken place in their lives. He said, "You are already clean because of the word I have spoken to you" (Jn 15:3). Yet, to make this change permanent, He assures them repeatedly that they should remain in Him. No change can remain and become permanent unless a Christian continues to have a relationship with the Father, the Son and the Holy Spirit. That relationship will remain fruitful, productive and clean. He continues in His discourse saying:

> No branch can bear fruit by itself; it must remain in the vine. Neither can you bear fruit unless you remain in me (Jn 15:4*b*).

As for the 'branches' of the vine, or the Christians, they are givers and receivers. They have duties to perform in order to receive the qualities of the 'True Vine'. They have to love Jesus as He loves them and to love one another. They have to remain connected to the vine in order to receive the nourishment; just as the branch that remains connected to the vine can continue to grow and produce grapes that are visible and useful. Jesus also explains the consequences of not abiding in Him. He said:

> If a man remains in me, and I in him, he will bear much fruit; apart from me you can do nothing. If anyone does not remain in me, he is like a branch that is thrown away and withers; such branches are picked up, thrown into the fire and burned (Jn 15:5*b*-6).

The change only becomes permanent when it is continuously nourished, cleansed and purified. Christians have to commit themselves to Jesus and not to let the world with its worries, lust and life style creep in. One has to be washed in the blood of the Lamb, to become one of His sheep.

Permanent change requires that we:
- trust that He is the Son of God (Mk 3:11),
- accept Him as Savior and Lord (Jn 1:12),
- accept the filling of the Holy Spirit (Jn 14:15-17),

- ask the Father for our needs (Jn 15:16*b*),
- obey Him (Jn 15:10), and
- remain in Him (Jn 15:7).

Jesus is the Way, the Truth and the Life, and no one comes to the Father except through Him. If someone chooses to go the other way, to disconnect himself with the Father and with the Son, that person will not belong to Him. Nothing can make this connection permanent more than love and obedience to God's commands. We have to cling to Him just as the branch clings closely to the vine for life and nutrition. If one part is disconnected, the whole branch may fall down by the power of the winds. Likewise is our relationship, if we choose not to remain in Jesus, to pray, to read His word, and to gospel to others about Him, we will end up disconnected to the source of eternal life, and die in the spirit. No joy is complete if we follow the world's pleasure. The only complete joy is in Jesus. He said, "I have told you this so that my joy may be in you and that your joy may be complete" (Jn 15:11).

One of the most promising fruits of the Spirit is that we become 'friends' of Jesus. We have become friends of Jesus because everything He had learned from the Father has been made known to us (Jn 15:15). It is such a blessing to remember how Abraham has always been called a 'friend' of God because he obeyed God as no other man did (Is 41:8). He was ready to sacrifice his son Isaac in obedience to God's command. Yet, the only one who *died* for our sins was

Jesus, who obeyed the Father to the point of crucifixion, as a testimony of love and sacrifice. Nothing matches this love and sacrifice.

The three key words in the discourse of the 'True Vine' are 'remain' (11 times), 'love' (9 times) and 'fruit' (8 times) (Jn 15:1-17).

Noteworthy, Jesus took the first step. He chose to love us and invited us to live with Him forever (Jn 15:16). What He asks is that we return this love to Him and love Him as He has loved us. The fruit of our love to Him is to love one another and to bear the fruit of the Spirit. Without that first step that He took, we would have never had the opportunity to choose to obey and love Him. When we live in Him, we:

- become a part of the body of Christ (Jn 15:5-6),
- are fruitful (Jn 15:5),
- love Him (Jn 13:34; 15: 2),
- love one another (Jn 13:34, 15:17), and
- share the complete joy we have in Him with others (Jn 15:11).

Transformation takes place when we accept Jesus as Lord and Savior. It is the work of the Holy Spirit. When this filling takes place, we grow into the likeness of Christ through the study of the Scripture and the constant relationship with Him. Prayer is of vital importance to our growth and fellowship with Him. The Scripture highlights the time Jesus spent in prayer and His advice that we pray unceasingly. We need to become the embodiment of Jesus. This likeness empowers us to serve and to minister to others.

One more aspect that is crucial for our lives as Christians is the filling of the Holy Spirit. Warren Benson[23] emphasizes the importance of the filling of the Holy Spirit, and the modeling of our ministries after Christ:

> Responding by total identification and by entrusting one's whole self to Jesus would be the height of folly and frustration except for the indwelling Spirit who enables us to achieve far greater similarity than any of us dream. The never-ending quest is to model our ministries after Christ, the supreme exemplar. He is the standard of all reflective valuation.

To sum up, the Master did not come to nullify the Law; He came to fulfill it. Nevertheless, the Orthodox traditions of the rabbis and teachers of the Law of His time did not comply with the Law. The rigidity of some of the Pharisees and the Scribes and the teachers of the Law made the situation extraordinarily complicated. Yet, the Master Teacher was seriously engaged in putting people back on the right track. His message is divine. He taught us that what defiles the soul is what comes out of a man such as theft, murder, lust, immorality, envy, slander, arrogance and folly. On the other hand, to those who surrender to Him and accept Him, He offers the free salvation that washes away their sins and cleanses the soul, mind and heart. It is a whole change. Remaining in Him makes this change permanent. This change is personal and individual. It is not limited to a certain age, nation, color or gender. It is a free gift offered to all who accept Him, for it is by grace that we are saved!

Chapter 6

A New Life

"A new command I give you: Love one another. As I have loved you, you must love one another. All men will know you are my disciples, if you love one another" (Jn 13:34-35).

Jesus called the first commandment a 'new command' whereas there was a similar commandment in the Old Testament that says:

> Do not seek revenge or bear a grudge against one of your people, but love your neighbor as yourself. I am the Lord (Lev 19:18).

Jesus called His commandment 'new' for several reasons. First, 'love one another' in the Old Testament was limited to 'love your people', or the Jewish community, but Jesus' command is love for everyone, with no discrimination among race, color, age, religion, denomination, affiliation, social status or health status, because everyone is united in Jesus.

Secondly, Jesus' commandment is 'new' because it has no boundaries. The Old Testament recommendation to 'love your neighbor as yourself' was undoubtedly great. Yet, Jesus' commandment has extremely high, long, deep, and broad dimensions that supersede any other love. Jesus said:

> ...as I have loved you, you must love one another (Jn 13:34*b*).

Thirdly, this commandment is 'new' because it is renewed and renewing with every new day and at all times. It is new because it is energizing to a Christian's activity and ability to give, forgive and endure.

Fourth, Jesus' commandment is 'new' because His love goes beyond any other love, as He tells us to love even our enemies. On His 'Sermon on the Mount', Jesus said:

> You have heard that it was said, 'Love your neighbor and hate your enemy'. But I tell you: Love your enemies and pray for those who persecute you, that you may be sons of your Father in heaven. He causes the sun to rise on the evil and the good, and sends rain on the righteous and unrighteous. If you love those who love you, what reward will you get? Are not the tax-collectors doing that? (Mt 5:43-46).

This love is unparalleled in any other religion. In fact, Mt 5:44 is the verse that recommends the love of enemies; it is a major factor that leads many people from other faiths to convert to Christianity. This love stands out as the most benevolent.

The fifth reason the Master calls this commandment 'new' is that it is permanent and everlasting. This new life in Jesus changes the heart and soul. It is the love that makes a person holy. It secures for a Christian a new life in Jesus on earth and eternal life with Jesus in heaven. To introduce the episode when Jesus washed His disciples' feet, the Apostle John documents:

> It was just before the Passover Feast. Jesus knew that the time had come for him to leave this world and go to the Father. Having loved his own who were in the world, he now showed them the full extent of his love (Jn 13:1).

The King James[24] translation says, "....Having loved his own which were in the world, he loved them unto the end".

In the phrase, "as I have loved you, you must love one another", Jesus sounds like He wants to say that all that He had done for us, was done for nothing other than love. Thinking of the great deeds that He has done for us, deeds that nobody else could have done, we realize how amazing His love is. Moreover, His love for us is not affected by our love for Him. He loved us first. Even if we do not return this love, and though we are not worthy of this love, He loves us still.

When He commanded us to love one another as He loved us, He recommended we do it even if the other party does not share this love, or seems to the world as unworthy. He has left for us a practical example to follow. As He did, we should do likewise.

The question arises: What did the Master's love look like? How can we describe it? What are its qualities, so that we can follow His example and live a new life in Him? Jesus' love for us is forgiving, sacrificing, permanent, understanding, selfless and productive.

Jesus' love is forgiving. The Master Teacher foretold the future about His betrayer to the disciples, while Judas Iscariot, the betrayer, who would turn Him over to authorities, was present (Jn 13:18). Yet, He never hated Judas. He forgave all His enemies at the time of severe agony on the cross when He said, "Father, forgive them; for they know not what they are doing" (Lk 23:34*a*). He also foretold that Peter would deny Him three times before the rooster would crow (Jn 13:38). Yet, He loved Peter and even chose Him to be the rock on which He would build His church. His forgiving love manifested itself when the angel told Mary Magdalene that Jesus had risen from the dead and said to her:

> But go tell his disciples and Peter, 'He is going ahead of you into Galilee. There you will see him, just as he told you' (Mk 17:7).

The Teaching of the Master

Although all of His disciples abandoned Him during the trial, Jesus did not hold grudges against them. He went to meet them in Galilee after His resurrection because He was looking forward to spending more time with them. Even those people, to whom He performed miracles, had all vanished. Where was Bartimaeus to whom Jesus restored his eyesight (Mk 10:52)? Where was Lazarus whom Jesus had raised from the dead (Jn 11-43)? Where were the lepers, the lame, and the demon-possessed whom Jesus had healed? Was there any one of the five thousand people whom He had fed with the two fish and five loaves (Mt 14:21)? His request from the Father to forgive those who hated or forsook Him included even the Gentile soldiers who had beaten and humiliated Him, as well as their fellow soldiers who nailed Him to the shameful cross. It is a matchless forgiving love. Jesus' forgiveness echoes what Micah said in the Old Testament:

> You will again have compassion on us; you will tread our sins underfoot and hurl all our iniquities into the depths of the sea (Mic 7:19).

The Master Teacher taught us forgiveness through His favorite method of teaching; parables. Peter had asked the Master if he [Peter] should forgive someone up to seven times. The Master answered him saying, "Not seven times, but seventy–seven times seven" (Mt 18:22*b*). Then Jesus told him the parable of the 'Unmerciful

Servant'. The king forgave one of his servants for a huge amount of debt he owed, but that servant went and punished his fellow servant who owed him a much smaller amount of money. In anger, the king turned the first servant over to the jailors until he could pay back what he owed the king (Mt 18:23-35). Likewise, God will forgive us if we repent, on condition that we forgive others. Jesus confirmed that by saying:

> For if you forgive men when they sin against you, your heavenly Father will also forgive you. But if you do not forgive men their sins, your Father will not forgive your sins (Mt 6:14-15).

The second feature in our new life that reflects Jesus' love is His sacrificial love. His sacrifice has no limits. The Son of God who knew no sin had to suffer emotionally and physically. He had to suffer emotionally from the blasphemy and abuse of the Pharisees and the Scribes, the false accusations of the High Priests and their illegal trial and the injustice and cruelty of the Roman rulers. He suffered emotionally when His own disciples either denied, or abandoned Him, at the time He most needed them. One of them, Judas, went so far as to turn Him over to the High Priest guards. He suffered physically during His ministry, as He had no place to rest His head (Lk 9:58). His enemies chased Him many times to kill Him. The Roman soldiers beat Him and spat on Him. He had to carry His heavy cross. He was crucified. He bled to death. Nevertheless, the Master's plan was to carry out the will of God for which He had come to earth. He loved us so much that He gave Himself to death so that whoever believes in Him would not die, but have eternal life (Jn 3:16). He focused on accomplishing His goal, regardless of any suffering or sacrifice. The writer of Hebrews recommends:

> Let us fix our eyes on Jesus, the author and perfecter of our faith, who for the joy set before him endured the cross, scorning its shame, and sat down at the right hand of the throne of God. Consider him who endured such opposition from sinful men so that you will not grow weary and lose heart (Heb 12:2-3).

Our new life in Jesus should have the essence of sacrifice of our own time, money and belongings. We should also counsel, minister, pray and support others in the spirit of love. Jesus considers that helping others and sacrificing for them is equal to doing the same for Him. He said in the parable of the 'Sheep and the Goats', referring to Himself as the 'king', "The king will reply, 'I tell you the truth, whatever you did for one of the least of these brothers of mine, you did for me'" (Mt 25:40).

Thirdly, Jesus' love is a discerning love. Jesus understood His disciples' strengths and weaknesses. He discerned their character and corresponding behavior. He knew very well that even though

Peter would deny Him during the trial (Jn 13:38), he would be the rock upon which He would build His church (Mt 16:18). He discerned that His disciple John loved Him profoundly (Jn 13:22). He foresaw that all of His disciples would forsake Him (Mt 26:31). Everything was clear and obvious to the Master, yet His discernment of others never diminished His love. He loved the righteous and the wicked, the clean and the unclean. He looked at people as the flock that needed the shepherd. The shepherd loves all the sheep and knows which sheep needs more care. He understands the nature of his sheep. He keeps trying to bring all his sheep into his sheep pen. At the same time, Jesus was fully aware of His enemies' mischief. The Pharisees and the Scribes attempted relentlessly to trap Him, but He understood their willful intentions and was able to confront them boldly.

In our new life in Him, Jesus wants us to love others with a discerning mind, to understand people's needs, behavior, character and intentions, in order to be able to help them grow spiritually. If we have Jesus in our lives, we will have constant fellowship with Him, recognize His voice, and accept His guidance. This is what Jesus does with us to day. We can address Him saying what David said in the Old Testament:

> O Lord, You have searched me and you know me. You know when I sit and when I rise; you perceive my thoughts from

afar. You discern my going out and my lying down. You are familiar with all my ways (Ps 139:1-3).

Warren Benson[25] explains the Master's discernment:

> As no other teacher, he being God (John 2:23-25), discerned men's and women's motivations as they approached him. This is the essence of the statement that none could ever teach as he did, in the ultimate sense of the term. However, he continues as the teacher whom we should study and examine more carefully because his teaching principles will never be outdated or become obsolete. Certainly, we have learned a considerable amount regarding the teaching-learning process since Jesus' day. And although the New Testament does not purport to be a manual on this process, it is remarkably contemporary, as a cursory examination of the biblical text will demonstrate.

Our love to others should not be affected negatively even if we are aware of their trespasses. Jesus understood sinners, yet He loved them. He loves us as is, the good and the not-so-good. Nevertheless, in our daily prayers, we renew our fellowship with Him, thank Him for His blessings and ask Him to make us whole and holy, to change us to be like Him.

The fourth quality of Jesus' love that can reshape our new life in Him is His permanent love. His love started since the creation of Adam and Eve, and will last forever. In the Old Testament we hear Him say, "Give thanks to the Lord for he is good and his love endures forever" (1Chr 16:34). When Jesus came to earth, He demonstrated His eternal love to us. The Apostle John emphasized Jesus' permanent love by writing, "Having loved his own who were in the world, he now showed them the full extent of his love" (Jn 13:1*b*). His love is free. It is given to us through grace, without merit, and forever for those who fear Him. The world gives us love, but that love is not the same like Jesus' love. Jesus treats us with so much gentleness and meekness although He is the King of kings. His love is always strong and can never be affected by outside influences, even if we do not return to Him the same love He has for us. Because His love is everlasting, we should love one another indefinitely, and with a pure heart. We can therefore confidently meet Him when He opens His arms to welcome us as the king in the parable of the 'Sheep and the Goats' welcomed his servants saying:

> 'Come you who are blessed by my Father, take your inheritance, the kingdom prepared for you since the creation of the world.... Then he will say to those on his left, 'Depart from me, you who are cursed, into the eternal fire prepared for the devil and his angels' (Mt 25:34, 41).

The fifth quality of our Master's love is His selfless love. Jesus' love is the noblest love. The Apostle Paul urges Christians to be like Jesus in selflessness and humility:

> Your attitude should be the same as that of Christ Jesus: Who, being in very nature God, did not consider equality with God something to be grasped, but made himself nothing, taking the very nature of a servant, being made in human likeness. And being found in appearance as a man, he humbled himself and became obedient to death - even death on a cross! (Phil 2:5-8).

To teach His disciples selfless love, The King of kings and Lord of lords washed the feet of His disciples. When Peter was reluctant to let the Master wash his feet, the Lord told him that if he would not let Him wash his feet, he [Peter] would not have part with Him (Jn 13:8*b*).

The sixth quality of our Master's love is His productive love. He is a man of action and production. In the incident of the 'fig tree', Jesus cursed the tree because it was fruitless. It had the appearance of a healthy tree, but it produced no fruit (Mt 21:18-19). Jesus started at an early age to be fruitful; to be of use to God and to people. Jesus did not only visit the sick and pray for them, He healed them. We can demonstrate our productive love by our gentle remarks, but more importantly by offering real help, by sharing our resources, time and effort to demonstrate this love. We read of the woman who demonstrated her love to Jesus by pouring an expensive perfume on His head (Mk 14:3-9) before His crucifixion, which He considered preparation for His burial. Jesus clearly tells us that whatever we do for the least of people, we do for Him.

Chapter 7

Blessed Assurance

"I have told you these things, so that in me you may have peace. In this world you will have trouble. But take heart! I have overcome the world" (Jn 16:33).

Jesus, the Master Teacher, the real Son of God, who calls us to live in reality, gives us this counsel: we will have discomforts in our life on earth, but to cheer up and rest assured, He has the world in His hands and consequently, He is able to handle our problems. Moreover, He considers that whoever hurts His people do, in fact, hurt Him. That applies to the same promise that God had given to His nation Israel through His prophet, ".... for whoever touches you, touches the apple of his [God's] eye" (Zech 2:8*b*). David also prayed to God saying, "Keep me as the apple of your eye; hide me in the shadow of your wings from the wicked who assail me, from my mortal enemies who surround me" (Ps 17:8-9).

Assurance is a combination of faith, confidence, trust and hope. The difference between faith and assurance is that faith precedes assurance: faith is trust that God can do things for us in the present time, while assurance is trust that God can do things for us in the future. Faith includes our expectation of receiving the blessings that God has promised us in our lifetime, whereas assurance means expectation of the fulfillment of what God has promised us for the future. Both faith and assurance have to do with the unseen. Although assurance foresees the future at a distance, it gives the strength to overcome difficulties in our present life. A close strong connection ties faith with assurance, for the stronger our faith is, the more assurance we have. Assurance can be identified as the product of strong faith. It can help us to do things or believe in things that, for an unbeliever, may seem insane.

Blessed assurance is a gift from God to man. He offers assurance to anyone who has opened his heart for God's word and has received Jesus as the Savior. During His life on earth, the Master Teacher gave assurance to all sorts of people, on different issues and occasions. His assurance focused mainly on ways to guarantee eternal life for each human being. In His glorious 'Sermon on the Mount', the Master Teacher focused on defusing our personal worries about physical necessities of life such as food, drink and clothes. Those concerns or worries not only demonstrate short sightedness and lack of faith, but they also block our assurance by building a wall that separates us from our heavenly Father who yearns to hear our voice.

The Master Teacher conveyed His divine message, making use of God's creation, such as birds and lilies that, most likely, were in view at the time He was speaking. He used the imperative forms of 'look' and 'see' to capture the visual as well as the auditory sense of His audience. On the aspect of worrying about food, He said:

> Look at the birds of the air; they do not sow or reap or store away in barns [as you do], and yet your heavenly Father feeds them. Are you not much more valuable than they? Who of you by worrying can add a single hour to his life? (Mt 6:26-27).

Furthermore, on the aspect of worrying on what to wear, He said:

> And why do you worry about your clothes? See how the lilies of the field grow. They do not labor or spin [as you do]. Yet I tell you that not even Solomon in all his splendor was dressed like one of these. If that is how God clothes the grass of the field, which is here today and tomorrow is thrown into the fire, will he not much more clothe you, O, you of little faith? (Mt 6:28-30).

Then Jesus concludes this part by stating the most important aspect of our life: prioritizing the needs of the soul. He asks us to rest assured that the Father is in charge of those physical necessities, whereas, we should focus on seeking the Father's kingdom:

> But seek first his kingdom and his righteousness, and all these things will be given to you as well (Mt 6:33).

In order for us to recognize God's assurance, we need to find out the source of assurance, the privilege of having it and the blessings because of having it.

The source of assurance is trust in God, remaining with God and being empowered by the Holy Spirit.

a) The first source of assurance is trust in God. Jesus revealed Himself as the Messiah to the Samaritan woman (Jn 4). She had committed many sins, and those sins had blocked her relationship with the real God. When she recognized Jesus, the Messiah, she voluntarily left her jar and rushed to her village to tell her fellow villagers about the good news. She abandoned everything and accepted the 'living water'. If we make a comparison between this woman and the rich young man who came to ask Jesus how he could inherit eternal life, we find a striking difference. The rich man refused to sell his possessions, to give the proceeds to the poor and follow Jesus. That man *left sadly* because he had many possessions (Lk 18:18-23). Less assurance results in less happiness: less assurance results in fewer blessings. The story of the poor widow provides a good example of the source of assurance:

> Jesus sat down opposite the place where the offerings were put and watched the crowd putting their money into the temple treasury. Many rich people threw in large amounts. But a poor widow came and put in two very small copper coins, worth only a fraction of a penny. Calling his disciples to him, Jesus said, 'I tell you the truth, this poor widow has put more into the treasury than all the others. They all gave out of their wealth; but she, out of her poverty, put in everything-all she had to live on' (Mk 12:41-44).

That poor woman could have had dire need for the money that she put in the collection box, but the trust she had that God could provide for her needs made her make a startling decision to offer all she had. Her present faith led her to have a strong assurance for the blessings of the future. The source of that assurance was her experience with God. She did not have a treasure on earth, but she had the confidence, hope and courage that led her to believe that she would certainly secure a treasure in heaven. She acted on her own will, *with satisfaction*. She probably wished that no one would have noticed her humble gift, but the Master's eyes were watching her with appreciation and admiration, to the extent that He shared His appreciation with His disciples. She praised God with her offering, and received praise from the Lord of lords. On the other hand, a person with less faith in God's power and mercy in the present will have less or no assurance for the future.

b) The second source of assurance is offered to us when we remain in God. This means that we have a solid pure relationship with God. In the parable of the 'True Vine', the Master Teacher assured His disciples:

> You are already clean because of the word I have spoken to you. Remain in me and I will remain in you (Jn 15:3-4*a*).

c) The third source of assurance is the filling of the Holy Spirit. The Master had promised His disciples, immediately before His ascension, that He would send the Holy Spirit (Lk 24:49). The Book of Acts documents the fulfillment of God's promise. On the day of Pentecost, as they assembled in one place, the Holy Spirit filled them (Acts 1:4, 2:1-4), and they started to spread the gospel to all nations.

Secondly, we have special privilege in Christian assurance:

a) The first privilege we have in Christian assurance is that it differs from human hope because it is a living hope. Our Master died on the cross for our sins. Yet, He rose victorious from the dead. He lives forever. He promised that where He would go, we would go also. He said:

> In my Father's house are many rooms; if it were not so, I would have told you. I am going there to prepare a place for

you. And if I go and prepare a place for you, I will come back and take you to be with me that you may be where I am. You know the way to the place where I am going (Jn 14:2-4).

b) The second privilege of God's assurance is the fact that it is glorious. Christ has prepared us for everlasting life. When Jesus told the rich ruler that it was easier for a camel to go through the eye of a needle than for a rich man to go to heaven, some people asked Jesus, "Who then can be saved?' Jesus replied, "What is impossible with men is possible with God" (Lk 18:26*b*-27).

c) Thirdly, God's assurance is blessed. God's blessings are abundant here on earth and in our future life. When the disciples stayed awake all night trying to catch *one* fish, they could not. Yet, when they put their trust in Jesus, they caught *plenty* of fish, The Scripture says, "When they had done so, they caught a large number of fish that their nets began to break" (Lk 5-6).

Thirdly, we are empowered by great blessings of assurance for the present and for the near and distant future.

a) The first blessing of assurance is peace (Jn 14:27). We can now walk our way in full and solid strides that can help us overcome all the difficulties that come our way. The receivers of blessed assurance are those who have overcome this life.

b) Another blessing of assurance is great joy. David always remembered God's assurance even at the darkest moments of his life. The Psalmist challenges his own sadness, "Why are you downcast, O my soul? Why so disturbed within me? Put your hope in God, for I will yet praise him, my Savior and my God" (Ps 42:5).

In His parable of the 'True Vine', the Master Teacher assured His disciples of the blessing of joy. He asked His disciples to remain in His love, by obeying His commands. He immediately mentioned joy. He said:

> I have told you this so that my joy may be in you and your joy may be complete (Jn 15: 11).

c) The third blessing of assurance is purity of heart and life. Our Master Teacher demonstrated for us the best example for purity. Moreover, He explained to us the roadmap with which we can tackle every angle in life. He taught us wisdom in our dealings with others, kindness to the needy, and love for one another, even our enemies. He gave His divine view on the sin of lust when He discussed adultery, quoting from the commandments, yet adding more holiness. He said:

> You have heard that it was said, 'Do not commit adultery'. But I tell you that anyone who looks at a woman lustfully has already committed adultery with her in his heart (Mt 5:27-28).

On the other hand, Jesus assured those who are pure in heart that they would be blessed by seeing God. He said in His astounding 'Sermon on the Mount':

> Blessed are the pure in heart, for they will see God (Mt 5:8).

d) The fourth blessing of assurance is patience and endurance: No cross; no crown. If we suffer with Him, we will be glorified with Him. The Master Teacher emphasized the fact that we would have troubles in this world, but He gave us assurance that makes our lives peaceful when we look up to Him. He said:

> I have told you these things so that in me you may have peace. In this world, you will have trouble. But take heart! I have overcome the world (Jn 16:33).

In His revelation to the Apostle John, Jesus repeated His assurance to those who would endure until the end. He gave assurance to the Church in Ephesus when He said:

> You have persevered and have endured hardships for my name, and have not grown weary…To him who overcomes, I will give the right to eat from the tree of life, which is in the paradise of God (Rev 2:3,7*b*).

e) Last, but not least is the blessing of complete salvation. Jesus' redemption is whole. It is a guarantee that our life is changed here on earth, and it will change into a glorious form when He welcomes us in His Father's house. We have become His own. The words that He said more than two thousand ago still echo with blessed assurance to all who have left everything and followed Him. On His second coming we can rest assured that He will say to each one of us, the believers:

> Well done, good and faithful servant! You have been faithful with a few things; I will put you in charge of many things. Come and share your master's happiness (Mt 25:21).

When the Master Teacher came to earth, His main goal was to save us from eternal hell. He, therefore, offered Himself on the cross to deliver us. Before He ascended to heaven, He gave us assurance about His Father's kingdom of heaven and the outpour of the Holy Spirit. Our life on earth is a preparation for eternal life with Him. In His teaching, He gave assurance using various tools, different literary forms, exciting parables, memorable discourses, healing miracles and prayers–all aimed at the future. Jesus said, "I am the way the truth and the life" (Jn 14:6*b*). He assured us, "Heaven and earth will pass away, but my words will never pass away" (Mt 24:35). We have seen many of God's promises fulfilled, and have full confidence in Him when He said:

Behold! I am coming soon! My reward is with me, and I will give to everyone according to what he has done (Rev 22:12).

Chapter 8

The Matchless Friend

"I no longer call you servants, because a servant does not know his master's business. Instead, I have called you friends, for everything that I learned from my Father I have made known to you" (Jn 15:15).

True friendship is a joy that each of us should cherish. It is one of the greatest gifts of God to humankind. If someone owns great wealth, or is famous for a great discovery, but has not been blessed by true friendship, that person's life would be dull and miserable. We have to raise thanks to God at all times for a true friend that shares our joy and sorrow, and we should always endeavor to extend that true friendship to our friends. Friendship does not last if it is not mutual. Friendship is giving and receiving; it is sharing and caring, sacrificing and enduring. Friendship is fun for the youth, a cane for the elderly and solace for the disressed.

The author of Proverbs 17 was inspired to write, "A friend loves at all times, and a brother is born for adversity" (Prov 17:17). This verse does not compare between a friend and a brother, or prefers one to the other; it rather praises the qualities of a real friend. Yet, the friendship of people could be temporary, when one of the friends leaves this world. It may also end during the lifetime due to any reason, such as long distance, lack of communication, selfishness, doubt and misunderstanding. It can also be undermined by a conflict of interest.

Jesus is the ideal and most faithful friend, at all times. In Him, we have the greatest friend of all. His friendship is matchless because it is strong and everlasting. Moreover, it has a great effect on our lives. He says:

> In the world you will have trouble. But take heart! I have overcome the world (Jn 16:33).

The Master's friendship is unique because it is permanent, captivating, transforming, sacrificing, understanding, and gentle.

It is a privilege to have Jesus as a friend, and the least we can do is to love Him because He loved us first, and He laid down His life for us. His friendship is permanent, endless and everlasting. It is not limited by time, circumstance, wealth or position. It has no discrimination. We just have to trust and believe on Him when He said:

Whoever believes in the Son has eternal life, but whoever rejects the Son will not see life, for God's wrath remains on him (Jn 3:36).

Secondly, Jesus' friendship is captivating. The Master has attracted people from all nations with His matchless love. When He spoke, the multitudes were mesmerized by His message of love and compassion, to the extent; they dismissed their basic need for food (Jn 6:5-12). People came in droves to hear His message and to be touched by His healing hand. No wonder that more than two thousand years later, His message continues to attract and amaze people.

Friendship with Jesus is transforming to our lives. He is a friend who can heal the body and the soul. The King of kings and Lord of lords is asking us to be His friends! He is able to raise us to the ranks of kings and priests. Friends usually have similar interests or qualities in common, prior to being friends. Yet, Jesus accepts us to be His friends because He can transform us to be like Him. In His teaching, the Master Teacher teaches us the ethics of the kingdom of heaven.

Fourthly, it is a privilege to be friends with the Master Teacher because He thinks of His followers before He thinks of Himself. His friendship is practical. He said in the parable of the 'True Vine', "Greater love has no one than this, that one lay down his life for his friends" (Jn 15:13). Moreover, the Master Teacher chooses His friends so that *He* can serve *them*; He has come to serve. Jesus sacrificed His own blood as a ransom for His friends. Moreover, we are assured of everlasting life with Him, if we obey His commands.

The Master's friendship is discerning and understanding. Although He knows our hearts and minds, He loves us. Yet, it is not a blind love. It is love with open eyes. He does not stand still when we sin but He warns and reprimands us. He confronts us with our shortcomings and helps us to get back on the right track. He tells us that if we choose to be like Him, we have to act worthily of His friendship, so that other people may see His light shine through us. He said:

> ...let your light shine before men, that they may see your good deeds and praise your Father in heaven (Mt 5:16*b*).

One more characteristic of Jesus' friendship is His gentleness. He said to His disciples, "Take my yoke upon you and learn from me, for I am gentle and humble at heart, and you will find rest for your souls" (Mt 11:29). In His 'Sermon on the Mount', He said, "Blessed are the meek, for they will inherit the earth" (Mt 5:5). His choice to be our friend is an overflow of modesty. One of the impressive scenes documented in the New Testament is of the Lord washing the feet of the disciples (Jn 13:4-8).

The amazing fact about Jesus' friendship is that He is interested in us and He expects us to return the same interest in Him. He is a friend who is there for us at all times and in all circumstances. He opens His arms and welcomes us whenever we are ready to accept Him. In human friendship, it is not easy to get people to be interested in you. Dale Carnegie[26] wrote:

> You can make more friends in two months by becoming interested in other people, than you can in two years by trying to get other people interested in you.

Jesus shows that joy and interest when we allow Him to enter into our hearts, and have interest in Him.

Introducing your friend to other people is one of the basic principles of courtesy; it shows love and respect. Likewise, if you have Jesus as your friend, He demands from you to introduce Him to others. He described His followers saying:

> You are the light of the world. A city on a hill cannot be hidden. Neither do people light a lamp and put it under a bowl. Instead they put it on its stand, and it gives light to everyone in the house (Mt 5:14-15).

In another situation, Jesus spoke more openly about not introducing Him, rather denying Him. He said:

> I tell you, whoever acknowledges me before men, the Son of Man will also acknowledge him before the angels of God.

> But he who disowns me before men, will be disowned before the angels of God (Lk 12:8-9).

Daniel Fuller wrote extensively about Abraham, the 'friend' of God. The Lord chose the elderly Abraham to leave Haran and go to Canaan, at the age of seventy-five. Abraham obeyed God, and therefore, God made a covenant with him. The Scripture honors that friendship. We read:

> But you, O Israel, my servant, Jacob, whom I have chosen, you descendents of Abraham, my friend, I took you from the ends of the earth from its farthest corners I called you (Isa 41:8-9a).

Although Abraham had come from a family of idolaters (Josh 24:2), he turned from the worship of gods to worship God. Nevertheless, Abraham was not without sin. Daniel Fuller[27] goes on to write about God's forgiveness to Abraham, God's friend:

> As Genesis 12-22 make clear, he [Abraham] did not become sinlessly perfect upon responding to the call, for from time to time he lapsed into great sins, the most notable of which were his twice selling his wife Sarah into a harem (Gen 12:11-15; 20:2). Yet, Abraham was forgiven, credited as righteous. On the occasion when this declaration was made,

> "[God] took Abraham outside [his tent], and said, 'Look up at the heavens and count the stars—if indeed you can count them.' Then he said to him, "So numerous shall your offspring be' (Gen 15:5). Then comes the declaration of forgiveness in verse 6.

When Abraham obeyed God, he was blessed. God promised that his descendents would be numerous as the stars in heaven, and He fulfilled His promise. When God asked him to offer his son Isaac as a sacrifice, he did not hesitate or question God (Gen 22:1-19).

As friends of Jesus, we are required to obey Him. Abraham could have made excuses not to obey God's command; he was seventy-five years old when God asked him to leave his country, and he was happy where he lived. When God commanded him to take his son and offer him as a sacrifice, he was definitely shocked, but never hesitated to obey God's orders. Abraham considered God's voice as an honor and a privilege. Jesus taught us how to recognize His voice and to follow His instructions even if they seemed not within our reach. The Master said, "You are my friends if you do what I command" (Jn 15:14).

One day Jesus chose to speak to the people from a ship belonging to Simon Peter. When He finished speaking, He told him to put out into deep water and to let down the nets for a catch. Simon answered:

Master, we've worked hard all night and haven't caught anything. But because you say so, I will let down the nets." When they had done so, they caught such a large number of fish that their nets began to break. So they signaled their partners in the other boat to come and help them, and they came and filled both boats so full that they began to sink. For he [Simon Peter] and all his companions were astonished at the catch of fish they had taken…..then Jesus said to Simon, 'Don't be afraid, from now on you will catch men.' So they pulled their boats up on shore, left everything and followed him (Lk 5:5-7, 9-11).

In the former quote from Luke, it is noteworthy that the fishermen had a hard time trying to catch fish. Then Jesus came onto the scene and asked them to go into deep waters, and let down their nets. They obeyed the Master, even though their obedience to go to deep sea and to let down their nets after so much toil might have seemed, to an unbelieving person, pointless or unwise.

Had they disobeyed the Lord, there would have been serious consequences. First, Jesus would not have chosen them as His disciples and they would have not become the apostles of Jesus who spread the word to the whole world. Secondly, they would have lost the blessings of being the Lord's friends. Thirdly, they would not have caught any fish, the source of income for many families represented in the two boats. Fourthly, they would have lived all their lives, occupied with the business of fishing, and not knowing about salvation. And finally, they would have missed the opportunity to share with their family members the great joy of knowing Jesus and obeying His commands.

Part III

Applications of the Master's Teaching

Chapter 9

Continued Fellowship

"....And I tell you that you are Peter and on this rock I will build my church, and the gates of Hades will not overcome it" (Mt 16:18).

The Master Teacher focused in His teaching on forming the listener's perception of the Father's kingdom. He explained, using parables and other literary forms, the significance of that kingdom and its crucial expectations. Throughout His teaching, the Master emphasized the effectiveness of the Golden Rule to His disciples: to love God, to continue in His love, and to love one another. He also commissioned His disciples to spread the gospel to all nations, baptizing them in the name of the Father and the Son and the Holy Spirit. In order for the Master Teacher to make His followers continue in fellowship with Him, He initiated the church, His body. Our Master Teacher was the first to use the word 'church', as documented twice in the Gospel of Matthew (16:18, 18:17). He also posed two extremely important questions to His disciples (Mt 16:13-20):

Question 1: *"Who do people say the Son of Man is?"* (v13*b*).
They replied: "Some say John the Baptist; others say Elijah; and still others, Jeremiah or one of the prophets" (v14).
Jesus made no comment. Yet, He made a follow-up question.

Question 2: *"But what about you?"* He asked, *"Who do you say I am?"* (v15).
Simon Peter answered: "You are the Christ, the Son of the living God" (v16).

Jesus commented:

> Blessed are you, Simon son of Jonah, for this was not revealed to you by man, but by my Father in heaven. And I tell you that you are Peter[28], and on this rock I will build my church, and the gates of Hades will not overcome it. I will give you the keys of the kingdom of heaven; whatever you bind on earth will be bound in heaven, and whatever you loose on earth will be loosed in heaven (vv. 17-19).

Jesus predicted the birth of the church and He commissioned His disciples not to leave Jerusalem until they would receive the Holy Spirit. Historically, the church was born in Jerusalem on Pentecost Day, a few days after Jesus' ascension to heaven.

In his first epistle, the Apostle John explains the aspect of 'fellowship'. The Apostle Paul also *discussed* fellowship several times in his epistles. Yet, it is Luke who documented in the Book of Acts, the initiation of the Christian church, and that helps us understand how the *fellowship* with Jesus *started* and *continued* after His ascension, and how it has developed and flourished to this day. Irving Jensen refers to Luke's faithful documentation of the *continued fellowship* in Christ. He summarizes the grand purposes on which the Book of Acts focuses: registration, *continuation* and propagation. On the aspect of *continued fellowship* in the Book of Acts, Jensen[29] writes:

> Luke's own words reveal this aspect of the narrative. His purpose in the third gospel was to record, like the writers before him, the origins of Christianity, "To compile an account of the things accomplished among us" (Luke 1:1). The first verse of Acts, by citing "all that Jesus began.....to do and teach" implies that Luke intends to show how Acts *continues* the story of Jesus as the ascended exalted One (Acts 1:2, 9).

The Teaching of the Master

The Book of Acts documents the new fellowship of the Christian believers after the filling of the Holy Spirit, as they are *all in one*. Jensen points out that Acts 2 documents the *continued fellowship and unity in the Spirit.* The Scripture[30] reads:

> (They) devoted (themselves) to the apostles' teaching and to the fellowship, to the breaking of bread and to prayer. (Everyone) was filled with awe and (many) wonders and miraculous signs were done by the apostles. (All) the believers were (together) and had (everything in common). Selling their possessions and goods, (they) gave to (anyone) as he had need. (Every day), (they) continued to meet (together) in the temple courts. (They) broke bread in their homes and ate (together) with glad and sincere hearts, praising God and enjoying the favor of (all) the people. And the Lord (added) to their numbers (daily) those who were being saved (Acts 2:42-47).

Kenneth Gangel[31] elaborates on *the* spirit of the first Christian church in Acts 2:

> At the end of Acts 2 we see the church as a devoted sharing and worshipping people (Acts 2:42-47). ……. Doctrine, fellowship, communion and prayer occupied their days and their devotion. They spent time together and shared common

goods to meet each other's needs. Verse 46 uses the word 'homothumadon', which appears eleven times in the New Testament, ten of which appear in the Book of Acts, it is the key word together (lit., "with one mind and purpose") and describes the attitude of those early believers.

During the days of the ministry of Christ, many people believed on Him, but with the outpour of the Holy Spirit, those invisible believers became members in the Christian church. The word 'church' (Greek *ekklesia*) is used in the New Testament to mean the Body of Christ. The Father's plan for redemption had been completed and the filling of the Holy Spirit had empowered the Christians with zeal and joy to spread the gospel to the whole world. The relationship between Christians developed into a new kind of relationship. There was then a new manifestation of the Holy Spirit in the newborn Christian church. Hence, early Christians' lives were changed due to the fruit of the Spirit, as the Apostle Paul declared, "But the fruit of the Spirit is love, joy, peace, patience, kindness, goodness, faithfulness, gentleness and self-control. Against such things there is no law" (Gal 5:22-23). The fellowship of the Father, the Son and the Holy Spirit had now sealed the hearts and souls of the Christian church. Donald Guthrie[32] wrote:

> As the Master Teacher, Christ presented good news about God, himself, his mission, the Holy Spirit, man and fellowship.

Irving Jensen[33] discussed the Persons of fellowship; the Father, the Son and the Holy Spirit, and the conditions of the fellowship as documented in the First Epistle of John:

> John also has much to say in his epistle concerning God the Father, whom he introduces in the opening paragraph (1:2-3). And when the apostle thinks about how Jesus the Son and God the Father are related to believers like himself, the first grand truth that comes to his mind is that of fellowship. The Son and the Father are the persons of the fellowship.

John explains in his first epistle how one can enjoy the full blessings of fellowship with God if one walks in the light (1Jn 1:5-7), confesses sin (1:8-10) and sins no more (2:1-2). Jesus' disciples, who were later called apostles, spread the ministry of Jesus Christ to the Jews and the Gentiles. The Christian church grew and multiplied. Alfred Edersheim[34] wrote on the union between Christ and the church, the union between Christ and His disciples, and the union of the disciples among themselves:

> The Union between Christ and His Church is *corporate, vital,* and *effective*, alike as regards and blessings (Jn 15:1-8). This Union issues in *Communion*-of Christ with His disciples, of His disciples with Him, and with His disciples among themselves. The principle of all of these is love: the love of Christ

to the disciples, the love of the disciples to Christ, and the love in Christ of the disciples to one another (Jn 15:9-17).

Nevertheless, there were positive as well as negative aspects. In the Book of Revelation, we treasure the Master's evaluation offered to His beloved Apostle John of the seven churches that were in Asia Minor[35] at that time. The Roman rulers in the Island of Patmos in Asia Minor put John in prison because He called on the name of Jesus. On the positive side, the letters to the churches of Ephesus, Smyrna, Pergamum, Thyatira, Sardis, Philadelphia and Laodicea consisted of Jesus' praise and acknowledgement, and the promised victory to those who continued fellowship with Him. On the negative side, Jesus enclosed His reprimand and warning to those churches that needed changes to continue in the fellowship of Christ. That evaluation needs our concern because it is a message from our Master for all the churches. It is also a mirror of what takes place in some of our churches today (Rev 2-3).

Jesus praised and acknowledged the seven churches in Asia Minor in the Book of Revelation for their:
   a) deeds, hard work and perseverance (2:2;3:7), although some lived where Satan had his throne (2:13)[36], for their truth and patience (2:19), doing more now than what was done first (2:2:19),
   b) intolerance of the church for the wicked men (2:3),

c) testing of those who claimed to be apostles (2:2),

d) perseverance of Jesus' name (2:2-3),

e) abstaining from the works of the Nicolaitans[37] (2:6),

f) suffering from poverty but being rich in the Spirit (2:9), and

g) remaining true to Jesus' name (2:10),

Jesus promised victory to those who would remain faithful and overcome until His second coming. He will:

a) give the right to eat from the tree of life which is in the paradise of God (2:7),

b) give the crown of life (to him who remains faithful, even to the point of death) (2:10),

c) give each to eat from the hidden manna (food of the Spirit), and will give a white stone with a new name to each, known only to those who receive it (2:17),

d) give to each authority to rule all the nations with an iron specter, and give to each the bright morning star (2:26, 27,

e) never erase their names from the book of life, but acknowledge their names before the Father and His angels (3:5),

f) make each of them a pillar in His Father's temple. He will write God's name on each of them as well as the name of the new Jerusalem (3:12), and

g) give each of them the right to sit with Him [Jesus] on His Father's throne (3:21).

On the other hand, ***Jesus reprimanded and warned*** the churches, through His Apostle John, against what He considered obstacles for a pure continued fellowship with Him. He addressed their shortcomings. They are those who:

a) had forsaken their first love to Jesus (2:4).

Warning: remember the height, from which they had fallen and repent (2:5).

b) were lenient with those who held the teachings of Balaam and the Nicolaitans (2:14).

Warning: repent; otherwise, Jesus would soon come to them with the sword in His mouth (2:16).

c) were lenient with Jezebel who called herself a prophetess and misled God's servants into sexual immorality (2:22).

Warning: Jesus gave Jezebel time to repent but she was unwilling. Therefore, Jesus would cast her in the bed of suffering and those who commit adultery with her would suffer intensely unless they repented (2:22-23).

d) had a reputation of being alive, but in fact were dead in the Spirit (3:14-20).

Warning: Jesus rebuked them to wake up, for Jesus found their deeds incomplete in the sight of God. He ordered them to remember and obey what they had received and heard. To repent; otherwise, Jesus would come like a thief at a time they would not know (3:3).

e) were liars in the Synagogue of Satan who claimed to be Jews (3:9).

Warning: Jesus would make them fall down and acknowledge that Jesus loved them (3:9).

f) were neither cold nor hot; because they were lukewarm, Jesus was about to spit them out of His mouth. They said they were rich, but they were wretched, pitiful, poor, blind and naked (3:16).

Warning: They should buy from Jesus gold refined by fire so they could get rich, and white clothes to wear so they could cover their shameful nakedness, and salve to put on their eyes so they could see (3:18).

Chapter 10

Personal Growth

"..Still, other seed fell on good soil. It came up and yielded a crop, a hundred times more than was sown" (Lk 8: 8).

Are you still growing physically? Have you reached maturity age? Are you growing in the spirit? Has your character developed? Has your love for God deepened? Do you spend some time with God on a daily basis for your spiritual growth? Do you speak to God? Are you thankful? Is your growth natural or forced? The Scripture tells us:

> And Jesus grew in wisdom and stature, and in favor with God and men (Lk 2:52).[38]

Likewise, a true Christian has to continue to grow, in order to be part of the whole body of Christ. A true Christian sees things in life as they are. Moreover, each believer does his or her best to solve any given problem, but leaves the rest to God. Submitting to God's will and taking advice from God's word, or from other Christians through the Holy Spirit, can enrich that growth.

Our Master Teacher presented the parable of 'The Sower' with its interpretation (Lk 8:5-8, 11-15). He used the seed to refer to the word of God, which fell on four types of cultivation soils referring to four types of people. He used the seed that fell along the path; it grew but was trampled by feet and eaten by the birds; to refer to those who hear the word, and then the devil takes away the word from their hearts. The second kind of seed fell among the rocks, referring to people who receive the word with joy, but they have no root. Therefore, when time of testing comes, they fall away. The third sample of seed was likened to the seed that fell among the thorns, referring to those who hear the word, but go on their way and are choked by life's worries, riches and pleasures, and do not mature.

The fourth type of seed, which the Master Teacher favors, is the one that falls on good soil. He explains:

> But the seed on good soil, stands for those with a noble good heart who hear the word, retain it, and by persevering produce a crop (Lk 8:15).

The Master Teacher wants His disciples, His followers, to grow. In order for a seed to grow and be fruitful, many factors work simultaneously: the seed, the soil, the sun and the water. In order for a Christian to grow, one needs to take some steps. Reading the Scripture on a daily basis is the first step in our spiritual growth, just like the water that nurtures the soil; without it, the plant would dry up and die. Secondly, daily prayer is vital for spiritual growth. Thirdly, using one's talents is an important step to enhance spiritual growth. The fourth step is to keep a healthy relationship with others. Moreover, having solid faith is the fifth step. Faith will help a Christian to grow and discover more power to follow the Great Commission. Jesus commanded His disciples before His ascension, saying:

> All authority in heaven and on earth has been given to me. Therefore, go and make disciples of all nations, baptizing them in the name of the Father and of the Son and of the Holy Spirit, and teaching them to obey every word that I have commanded you. And surely, I will be with you always, to the very end of the age (Mt 28:18*b*-20).

On the other hand, there are obstacles that hinder our growth. The first obstacle is lack of knowledge of the Scripture and the prophecies. The Master Teacher likened that sample of people to the seed that fell along the path, was trampled by men's feet, and then eaten by the birds. Secondly, the Master Teacher used the rocks as a metaphor for rigidity of some people, or having no root. Rigidity is one of the most misleading characteristics for a Christian. The Pharisees' failure to accept Jesus was due in part to their rigidity in accepting the new faith. They stuck to their own principles, which either their rabbis taught them, or through their own misinterpretation of God's word. Another obstacle is not obeying God's first Commandment: Love God, and love your neighbor as yourself. Drifting away or loving the world with its pleasures will eventually make a person die spiritually, such as the seed that produced a plant, but the thorns choked it. A fourth type of people does not have any problem other than impatience, or lack of perseverance, to continue to grow and help others grow.

There are characteristics of growth in the Spirit. It does not stop even if a person has reached maturity age. Growth develops the character of the Christian believer who is enriched through the word of God written in the Scripture. Another characteristic of growth is the development of a thankful heart in the Christian, a positive attitude towards God and towards people. It is a natural, not artificial or forced growth. Moreover, a good Christian believes in God's supernatural power. Stephen Arterburn[39] gave some valuable insights on the growth process:

> We must not demand instant change and quick fixes from those who find their way to Christ. We must allow for a process of transformation and growth. When Christ delivers someone from a sin, he [does not] usually deliver him or

her instantly into character. Character takes time to build and grow. God asks us to be patient with his people. [Let us] allow him to change them through the power of the Holy Spirit. He can accomplish through love and divine wisdom what we can never change through wagging our heads and pointing our fingers.

Growing also involves our trust in Jesus' power to do miracles in our daily lives. Miracles do happen, yet skeptics would argue that the era of miracles has ceased with the end of Jesus' life on earth. In order to grow, we have to believe and not doubt. Jesus does not require lots of faith to start the growth process. When the disciples could not heal the epileptic boy, the Scripture says:

> Then the disciples came to Jesus in private and asked, "Why couldn't we drive it out?" He replied, "Because you have so little faith. I tell you the truth, if you have faith as small as a mustard seed, you can say to this mountain, 'Move from here to there' and it will move. Nothing will be impossible for you!" (Mt 17:19-21).

When a Christian works with people, that person needs to explain to them that they should die not only to the Law but also to themselves. Henry Cloud[40] considers that true growth begins with realizing that we are poor in the Spirit, and from this humble position one reaches out to God and receives all that He has for us. He wrote:

> What helped people grow involved paths of growth I had never been taught in all of my Christian growth training or in my own spiritual life. It involved deep transformations of the soul that I had never seen.

Before trying to counsel other Christians to grow, one first has to grow personally. It is noticeable, in that respect, that in the last four decades, the church has become more and more involved in individual growth as well as in members' social concerns. Family and youth fellowships have grown. Prayers, visits, and support group involvement drew people closer to solve spiritual and social issues. Yet, there is more need for closer Bible study that enriches our souls and develops our relationship with God. Biblical doctrines should go side by side with growth in our spiritual relationship with God. Some of the doctrines that apply to growth are being offered in Bible Study, in learning about the Father, the Person of Christ and the Holy Spirit. In addition, in order for a Christian to grow, one should study the role of truth and grace, the role of sin and temptation, the role of the church, poverty of spirit and sadness, sin and forgiveness, confession, discipline and correction, obedience and repentance, pain and suffering.

Growing spiritually is the best solution for one's problems. Spiritual growth is crucial and indispensable for Christians to live the divine life that is the road to the kingdom of God. The Master Teacher said:

> But seek first his kingdom and his righteousness and all these things will be given to you as well (Mt 6:33).

In our relationship with God, we cannot grow on our own, but we have to yield our lives to Him who created us. He will lead us to success and enable us to invest in ourselves, and in others. The Bible informs us of the process through which people grow. In Jesus, we have the practical model of personal and spiritual growth.

If you are a teacher that helps people grow, you are God's ambassador. You have already accepted to let Him dwell in your heart and, therefore, He personally makes changes in your life. In Jesus' 'Great Commission' to His disciples [us], He promises to be with us always (Mt 28:16-20). He does not expect that life will be easy for us. He has suffered on earth to the point of death and He told us that we would suffer for His name. In the Epistle of James we find that it is a privilege and a joy to suffer for Jesus:

> Consider it pure joy, my brothers, whenever you face trials of many kinds, because you know that the testing of your faith develops perseverance (James 1:2 3).

James continues in verse 4, "perseverance must finish its work so that you may be mature and complete, not lacking anything." Rick Warren[41] commented on the above quote, saying:

> Notice again that 'joy' comes 'because you know'. It is always a matter of perspective.

In order to develop spiritually, we must seek fellowship with others. We can learn of fellowship from those who were contemporaries of Jesus, as well as from any Christian person from the days of Jesus to this day. First, Christians rejoice even in times of tragedy and trial because God has purpose in their lives. Secondly, Christians have joy because perseverance produces perspective. A third reason why fellowship produces joy is that we are reconciled with God. The Scripture says, "...we also rejoice in God through our Lord Jesus Christ, through whom we have now received reconciliation" (Rom 5:11*b*).

In Isaiah 43:2, we hear the echo of this great hope: "When you pass through the waters, I will be with you; and when you pass through the rivers, they will not sweep over you. When you walk through the fire, you will not be burned; the flames will not set you ablaze."

In your fellowship with Jesus, you can definitely develop spiritual growth on a daily basis. The disciples grew spiritually even though no disciple of Jesus had a theological background. Yet, they became the pillars of Christianity who willingly spread the gospel to the whole world. Their growth was overwhelming. Lee Magness[42] wrote:

> For the disciples, learning was living, living with and like Jesus. Perhaps we should interpret more literally; Learning was becoming, being like Jesus. Education in Christ was not even merely the mimicry of Jesus' habits; it was growth into a state of being which was Christ-like.

Chapter 11

Sharing the Gospel

"Then Jesus came to them and said, "All authority in heaven and on earth has been given to me. Therefore, go and make disciples of all nations, baptizing them in the name of the Father and of the Son and of the Holy Spirit, and teaching them to obey everything I have commanded you" (Mt 28:18-19).

Early in His ministry, the Master Teacher was walking beside the Sea of Galilee. He saw Simon and his brother Andrew casting a net into the lake, for they were fishermen. "Come, follow me," Jesus said, "and I will make you fishers of men" (Mt 4:19; Mk 1:17). After selecting the twelve, He trained them throughout the time He ministered on earth. His master plan was to fully train them before sending them out to share the gospel with all humankind. The Scripture also documents that Jesus sent them two by two to share the gospel. He ordained them to teach, preach, baptize, heal and cast out evil spirits. We read in the Gospel of Mark:

> Then Jesus went around teaching from village to village. Calling the twelve to him, he sent them out two by two, and gave them authority over evil spirits (Mk 6:7).

Jesus gave them important instructions that are crucial for our endeavor today to spread the gospel (Mk 6:8-13, 30). He gave them the following commands:

a) Take nothing for the journey except a staff.
b) Take no bread, bag, or money.
c) Wear sandals.
d) Do not wear an extra coat.
e) Whenever you enter a house, stay there until you leave the town.
f) If any place will not welcome you, or listen to you, shake the dust off your feet when you leave, as a testimony against them.
g) Pray.

The Master Teacher had 'rigorous demands' from His disciples, because He wanted them to grow in the Spirit. In that respect, Warren Benson[43] wrote:

> His [Jesus'] rigorous demands of the disciples called for the very best that was in them. He encouraged them to grow and to try out the same techniques he used in ministry. Eventually, this involvement in learning caused them to stand sturdily for the truth when Christ ascended to heaven.

The mission of the disciples was successful. The Scripture documents, "They went out and preached that people should repent. They drove out many demons and anointed many sick people with oil and healed them" (Mk 6:12-13). When they came back, we read, "The apostles gathered around Jesus and reported to him all that they had done and taught" (v. 30). Although the disciples' ministry was not always smooth and their faith was not always solid, they certainly learned from their experiences. The Scripture documents one incident when the disciples were not up for the task. It was the incident of the healing of a boy with an evil spirit. Jesus saw a huge crowd and heard arguments between His disciples and some teachers of the Law. When He inquired about that matter, a man in the crowd told the Master that an evil spirit possessed his son since childhood, and he had brought him to the disciples to heal him but they could not. (Mk 9: 14-29). Jesus healed the boy. Later, when the disciples were indoors with Jesus, they asked Him, "Why couldn't we drive it out?" He replied, "This kind can come out only by prayer" (vv. 28-29).

The Teaching of the Master

After Jesus' crucifixion and burial, the eleven surviving disciples went to Galilee as Jesus had commanded them. When they saw Him there, after His resurrection, they worshipped Him, although some of them doubted. Before His ascension, Jesus instructed them not to leave Jerusalem until they received the Holy Spirit. He then commanded them to go and make disciples of all nations, and baptize them in the name of the Father, and of the Son and of the Holy Spirit.

Sharing the gospel with others is one of the results of salvation through the blood of Jesus. No one can light a candle and hide it, expecting it to give light. Jesus said to His disciples in His 'Sermon on the Mount', "You are the light of the world" (Mt 5:14*a*). Jesus did not leave His disciples in the dark. In His teaching, Jesus shared the gospel with His disciples in at least three aspects that ascend in endurance. He taught them how to share the gospel, what to expect in their ministry and who to minister to.

The first aspect we learn from the teaching of the Master is that we will reap the harvest of the seed that we have *not* sown. Jesus said to His disciples, after the salvation of the Samaritan woman:

> Thus the saying 'One sows and another reaps' is true. I sent you to reap what you have not worked for. Others have done the hard work, and you have reaped the benefits of their labor (Jn 4:37-38; Mic 6:15).

Jesus had sown the seed and the disciples could reap the harvest of believers of the early church. The Christian church multiplied generation after generation. Yet, the One who did the hard work was the Savior who shed His blood to save us. Jesus commands us to spread the word; to gospel to others of the mercies of God's love. The Samaritan woman started one of the very early ministries of Christ. She was able to share the gospel with her fellow villagers in the whole town of Sychar. She reaped for what she did not work. Jesus can use even the lowliest of people, like the Samaritan woman, to share the miraculous gift of God. David Mckenna[44] observes:

> Jesus took a major risk with the persons he chose to be his disciples. None of them was theologically sophisticated, trained for leadership or primed for a public image. Yet, strange as it seems, Jesus chose them for their independence, diversity, and non-conformity. But in the long-run, their differences could be their strengths.

The second aspect of sharing the gospel is ministry that is full of personal sacrifices. The Scripture documents about the Samaritan woman, "….Then leaving her water jar, the woman went back to her town and said to the people, 'Come, see a man who told me everything I ever did. Could that be the Christ?'" (Jn 4:28-29). Yet, sharing the gospel with others is not always easy. In fact, Jesus taught us in the Olivet Discourse with His disciples about the persecution, the whipping and even the possible killing of whosoever gospels in His name. In the Old Testament, the Psalmist was inspired to write that whatever we sow in tears we will reap in joy, "He who goes out weeping, carrying seed to sow, will return with songs of joy, carrying sheaves with him" (Ps 126:6). The bliss that the gospel sharer enjoys will wipe out all the shed tears through the ministry journey, even if one soul is saved. Jesus also said:

> There is rejoicing in the presence of the angels of God over one sinner who repents (Lk 15:10*b*).

The third aspect of sharing the gospel is the hardest. Jesus explained it by the seed that has to die in the ground in order to grow and produce many seeds. One seed of wheat may grow to give more than thirty seeds in one spike. Jesus said:

> I tell you the truth, unless a kernel of wheat falls to the ground and dies, it remains a single seed. But, if it dies, it produces many seeds. The man who loves his life will lose it, while the man who hates his life in the world will keep it for eternal life (Jn 12:24-25).

Therefore, in order to become a disciple of Jesus, each one has to deny himself, die **to** the world, and follow Him.

Unlike the traditional Jews of that time, Jesus and His disciples knew no boundaries. They interacted with the Gentiles in spite of the language barriers, difference in religion, culture and tradition. The Pharisees had fiercely criticized Jesus, for sitting with sinners and those that they considered unclean, such as the Gentiles. Yet Jesus' mission was for the whole world. He came to rescue the 'lost sheep'. The Master knew no discrimination. He had come for His own, but His own did not accept Him. Therefore, He turned to the others, the Gentiles, and offered eternal life to each one who accepted Him. His disciples followed in His footsteps. After His ascension, they preached in the synagogues, but when they were not accepted, they spread the good news to the other nations. Alfred Edersheim[45] wrote on the union between Christ, His disciples and the church, and how that union commands us to separate ourselves from the world in a unique manner:

> This Union and Communion has for its necessary counterpart Disunion, Separation from the world. The world repudiates them [gospel sharers] for their Union with Christ and their Communion. But, for all that, there is something that must keep them from going out of the world. They have a mission in it, initiated by, and carried on in the power of the Holy Ghost - that of uplifting the testimony of Christ (Jn 15:18-27).

Christ's Great Commission to His disciples, when He was at the point of leaving this earth and going to the Father, is extremely powerful and loaded with action and commitment followed by His blessed assurance to the disciples [followers] (Mt 28:18-20):

Commission:
a) Go to all nations.
b) Make disciples of all nations.
c) Baptize the disciples of all nations.
d) Teach the disciples to obey my commands.

Blessed assurance:
a) All authority in heaven and earth is given to me.
b) I will be with you always, to the very end of the age.

Chapter 12

Accomplished Mission

"…..his master replied, 'Well done, good and faithful servant! You have been faithful with a few things; I will put you in charge of many things. Come and share your master's happiness!'"(Mt 25:21).

During the Olivet Discourse, the Master Teacher gave three parables about the kingdom of heaven and His second coming. The parable of 'The Ten Virgins' (Mt 25:1-13) was meant to illustrate preparedness for His coming. As for the second parable on 'The Talents' (Mt 25:14-30), the Master Teacher's message was about the accomplished mission. The third parable 'The Sheep and the Goats' was geared towards the Day of Judgment (Mt 25:31-46).

In the parable of 'The Talents'[46], the owner of the property distributed his wealth (talents) among his servants. He tasked them to invest in those talents. He did not give them an equal number of talents, because he was their master and was aware of each one's ability. He did not give any of them more than what they could handle. He gave one of them five talents, to the second servant he gave two talents and to the third, he gave one talent. He asked them to invest in that money until he would come back from his long trip. In other words, he gave them enough time to invest their talents. The servant with the five talents worked so hard and doubled the five talents. The second servant with two talents also doubled them. The two servants showed their faithfulness to their master and had assurance that he would reward them for a job well done. As for the third servant, he dug a hole in the ground and hid the talent, making no investment. He made his excuse:

> 'Master', he said, 'I knew that you are a hard man, harvesting where you have not sown and gathering where you have not scattered seed. So I was afraid and went out and hid your talent in the ground. See, here is what belongs to you' (Mt 25:24*b*-25).

Unfortunately, he blamed his master for his own lack of action. 'Talent' here refers to any source of strength such as money, a gift, ability or knowledge. Given that source of strength or strengths, God offers us time to allow us to invest in those strengths. He expects us to utilize them wisely. The main issue, therefore, is not how much we have, but how much we do with what we have, to accomplish our mission and fulfill it to God's satisfaction.

After God had created the world in six days, He rested on the seventh day. The Hebrew translation for 'rested' is 'completed'. God had the sense of completion, not weariness (Gen 2:2). God also had the sense of satisfaction, when, in the process of creation, He saw that His creation was good. God's satisfaction and sense of accomplishment could not be complete until He found that humans have this need-love for Him. Adam and Eve did not give Him that satisfaction, nor all the generations that followed. Therefore, God sent His only Son, Jesus Christ, to save us from our sins. Jesus said on the cross before He died, "It is finished" referring to the plan God had set for Him (Jn 19:30*b*). The crucified Christ carried all the sins of the world. He "finished" His mission and had a sense of completion and satisfaction when it was done.

The master in the parable of 'The Talents' who came back after a long time refers to Jesus' second coming. The Lord Jesus will return. We know that for a certainty. We learn from the above parable to focus not only on serving the Lord; but also to use our time, resource and talent to serve Him completely in what we do. That service may include helping people or may require changing a job, location or destination, but for most of us, it means performing our mission with the desire to love God and to love one's neighbor as oneself.

The master in the parable of the 'Talents' gave the servants different amounts of talents, but because both of the first two worked hard to do their best to serve the master they loved, their master was equally happy with them. He expressed his great satisfaction and rewarded both of them, when he said to each of them:

> Well done, good and faithful servant! You have been faithful with a few things; I will put you in charge of many things. Come and share your master's happiness (Mt 25:21).

The hour of delivering Jesus to the hands of the leaders was drawing near, and Jesus had a sense of dedication before He ended the Olivet Discourse: to make the picture perfect about 'The Kingdom of Heaven'. The parable of 'The Sheep and the Goats' followed the parable of 'The Talents' immediately. The Sheep and the Goats illustrated the fulfillment of the master's promise to share his happiness with those who have accomplished their mission. In that parable, the Master Teacher was more specific when He said:

> When the Son of Man comes in his glory, and all the angels with him, he will sit on his throne in heavenly glory. All the nations will be gathered before him and he will separate the people one from another as a shepherd separates the sheep from the goats (Mt 25:31-32).

On His second coming, the Master Teacher will assume the role of the Judge. He will put the sheep (righteous) on the right and the goats (sinners) on the left. Each will be judged according to what one did or did not do.

Following the same steps of our Lord, we are required to work hard in His vine in order to redeem the time because of the evil times that we live in. There is a lot of work to do in this vine but the workers are not so many. If we choose to do it ourselves, not to disciple others, then the word of God will diminish. Yet, any honest disciple of the Master will agree with the writer of Hebrews, as inspired by the Holy Spirit, about the word of God:

> For the word of God is living and active. Sharper than any double-edged sword, it penetrates even to dividing soul and spirit, joint and marrow; it judges the thoughts and attitudes of the heart (Heb 4:12).

The three major religions of Judaism, Christianity and Islam deal with the issue of the end of the world, although they differ in explaining it. Yet, the three Synoptic Gospels all agree concerning Jesus' discourse on the end of the world (Mt 24; Mk13; Lk 21:5-36). Jesus described the tribulations, wars and human sorrows that would precede such an unequaled event. He spoke of "the day" in reference to two things: The first was the 'Destruction of Jerusalem' that took place in A.D. 70.[47] The second was the final and consummate 'Day of the Lord' that believers are looking forward to. To illustrate these two crucial events, Philip Hughes[48] wrote:

While, however, the events of A.D. 70 were invested with the most portentous significance (cf. Matthew 24), and in the prophetic prospective, there could be lesser "days of the Lord" which pointed to the certainty of the ultimate day of judgment "the Day", without any qualification, and therefore, emphatic in the absoluteness of its significance, must be the day of Christ's return when this present age will be brought to its conclusion and his everlasting kingdom over the new heaven and the new earth universally established.

Nearly two millenniums have passed and 'the Day' has not come yet. The prophecies of Jesus' first coming had seemed to the Jews extremely delayed in their fulfillment, likewise Jesus' second coming. Yet, His second coming becomes more and more confirmed when signs begin to take place. The period between the first coming of Christ and His 'parousia' marks the 'end time', the 'last days' and the 'last hour'.

No book in the Bible, has given us a better preview of heaven and hell than John's Book of Revelation. R. C. Sproul[49] calls it "the Apocalypse of the New Testament". Its symbolic literary form, style, and numeric references make it stand out as one of the most divine declarations from God that announces the second coming of Jesus, and the details of such coming.

The question arises: are we prepared for Jesus' coming? Have we accomplished our mission on earth? Are we reminded of the general impression when He comes that there will be no time to do anything? The Master Teacher divinely answered those questions to help us understand the element of time we have when He comes. He said:

> Let no one in the field go back to get his cloak. How dreadful will it be in those days for pregnant women and nursing mothers! Pray that your flight will not take place in winter or on the Sabbath. For then, there will be great distress, unequaled from the beginning of the world until now - and never to be equaled again (Mt 24:18-21).

The issue of chronology in the Bible is worth mentioning as it involves many events that are of crucial concern to us. As for the prophets of the Old Testament, they viewed their prophecies as happening in the near future. The same can be said about the Book of Revelation. According to Kenneth Gentry[50], the use of three words that appeared frequently refer to events taking place in the [near] future. He identifies the seven times repetition in the letters to the churches in the Book of Revelation in the opening and closing chapters and three more times in the letters in chapters two and three. He classifies those words referring to the future in three word groups:

The first word-group is the 'taxos' group, usually translated as 'soon' or 'shortly' (Rev 1:1; 2:16; 3:11; 22:6, 7, 12, 20).

The second word-group is the 'engus' group, usually translated as 'near' or 'at hand' (Rev 1:3; 22:10).

The third word-group is 'mello'. It is a verb translated as 'destined', yet Gentry believes that when used in Revelation, it meant 'to be on the point of' or 'to be about to' (Rev 1:19; 3:10). As a result, in his doctoral dissertation, Gentry concluded that John used the above-mentioned word groups because he wrote the Revelation before the destruction of Jerusalem (before A.D. 70). Some scholars follow the same school such as Adam Clarke and Henry Barclay. Other scholars, such as Irenaeus and Clement of Alexandria stated that it was written after A.D. 70. Irving Jensen also belongs to that school and he believes that John was inspired by God to write Revelation around A.D. 96.

No one knows when the second coming of Jesus will take place. In answer to the disciples' question about His second coming, Jesus said:

> So if any one tells you, 'There he is, out in the desert', do not go out; or, 'Here he is, in the inner rooms', do not believe it. For as the lightning comes from the east and flashes to the west, so will be the coming of the Son of Man. Wherever there is a carcass, there the vultures will gather. Immediately after the distress of those days,' the sun will be darkened, and the moon will not give its light; the stars will fall from the sky, and the heavenly bodies will be shaken (Mt 24:26 27).

There are three stages of the resurrection, but the Scripture says, "For the sake of the elect, those days will be shortened" (Mt 24:22).

The first stage is the resurrection of Christ that is marked by the resurrection of the dead. Jesus' Messianic reign began after His resurrection because His kingdom was "not of this world" (Jn 18: 36).

The second stage is the pre-end of the age of saints. It is the completion of the first stage.

The third stage is the universal resurrection that is confirmed in Matthew 24:3-8, 14.

The mission has been accomplished! Those who have **accepted Jesus Christ as their personal Savior, and followed the Master Teacher's teachings** on earth are worthy of being in the presence of the Master, the Lord of lords, and share the everlasting happiness.

Bibliography

- Gangel, Kenneth D. "What Christian Education Is", in <u>Christian Education: Foundations for the Future</u>, Robert Clark *et al*, editors. (Chicago: Moody Press, 1991).
- Gentry, Kenneth L, Jr. <u>The Beast of Revelation.</u> (Tyler: Institute for Christian Economics, 1989).
- Guthrie, Donald. "Jesus" in <u>A history of Religious Educators</u>, Elmer E. Towns, *ed*. (Grand Rapids: Baker, 1975).
- Henry, Matthew. <u>Commentary on the Whole Bible</u>. (Peabody: Hendrickson, 1991).
- Hinn, Benny. <u>The Anointing</u>. (Nashville, Thomas Nelson Publishers, 1992).
- Hughes, Philip E. <u>A Commentary on the Epistle to the Hebrews</u>. (Grand Rapids: Eerdmans, 1977).
- Jensen, Irving L. <u>Jensen's Survey of the Old Testament</u>. (Chicago; Moody Bible Institute, 1978).

- Jensen, Irving L. *Jensen's Survey of the New Testament*. (Chicago; Moody Bible Institute, 1981).
- Knight, George W. *The New Testament Teaching on the Role Relationship of Men and Women.* (Grand Rapids: Baker Book House, 1977).
- Kuhlman, Edward. *Master Teacher.* (Old Tappan: Revell, 1987).
- Mckenna, David. *Power to Follow, Grace to Lead*. (Florida: W. Pub Group, 1989).
- Magness, Lee. "Teaching and Learning in the Gospels: The Biblical Basis of Christian Education", *Religious Education 70*, no 6 (November-December, 1975): 629-35.
- Pazimo, Robert W. *Foundational Issues in Christian Education*. (Grand Rapids: Baker Books, 2004).
- Richards, Lawrence O. *Expository Dictionary of Bible Words*. (Grand Rapids: Zondervan, 1985).
- Sproul, R.C. *The Last Days According to Jesus,* 7th ed. (Grand Rapids: Baker Books, 2007).
- Stein, Robert H. *Jesus the Messiah: A Survey of the Life of Christ*. (Downers Grove, Inter-Varsity Press, 1996).
- Strobel, Lee. *The Case for Christ,* (Grand Rapids: Zondervan Publishing House, 1998).
- Trueblood, Elton D. *The Lord's Prayer*. (New York: Harper & Row, 1965).
- Warren, Rick. *God Power to Change Your Life*. (Grand Rapids: Zondervan, 2006).

Bible Versions

- New International Version. (Grand Rapids: Zondervan, 1983).
- King James Version, *with concordance*. (American Bible Society: New York, 1963).

Endnotes

[1] Jensen Irving L. <u>Jensen's Survey of the New Testament,</u> (Chicago: Moody Press, 1981), p. 112.

[2] Fuller, Daniel P. <u>The Unity of the Bible</u>. Grand Rapids: Zondervan, 1992), p. 135.

[3] Fuller, Daniel P. <u>The Unity of the Bible</u>. Grand Rapids: Zondervan, 1992), p. 139.

[4] Friedman, Matt. <u>The Master Plan of Teaching</u>. (Wheaton: Victor, 1990), pp. 21-30.

[5] Benson, Warren S. "Christ the Master Teacher" in <u>Christian Education-Foundations for the Future</u>, Robert Clark *et al* (editors). (Chicago: Moody, 1991), pp. 88-9.

[6] Mckenna, David. <u>Power to Follow, Grace to Lead</u>. (Florida: W. Pub Group, 1989), pp. 22-23.

[7] Trueblood, Elton D. <u>The Lord's Prayer</u>. (New York: Harper & Row, 1965), p. 36.

[8] Freidman, Matt. <u>The Master Plan of Teaching.</u> (Wheaton: Victor, 1990), pp. 21-30.

[9] Jensen Irving L. <u>Jensen's Survey of the New Testament.</u> (Chicago: Moody Press, 1981), p. 169.

[10] New Living Bible. Daily Study Bible for Women. Wheaton: Tyndale House Publishers, 1999).

[11] Guthrie, Donald. "Jesus" in <u>A history of Religious Educators,</u> Elmer L. Town, *ed.* (Grand Rapids: Baker, 1975), pp. 26-35.

[12] Kuhlman, Edward. <u>Master Teacher.</u> (Old Tappan: Revell, 1987), p.181.

[13] Benson, Warren S. "Christ the Master Teacher" in <u>Christian Education: Foundations for the Future</u>. Robert Clark *et al* (editors). (Chicago: Victor, 1991), p. 88.

[14] Benson, Warren S. "Christ the Master Teacher" in <u>Christian Education: Foundations for the Future</u>. Robert Clark *et al* (editors). (Chicago: Victor, 1991), p. 88.

[15] Benson, Warren S. "Christ the Master Teacher" in <u>Christian Education: Foundations for the Future</u>. Robert E. Clark *et al, editors*. (Chicago: Moody Press, 1991), p. 94.

[16] Stein Robert H. <u>Jesus the Messiah, A Survey of the Life of Jesus</u>. (Downers Grove: Intervarsity, 1996). p. 123.

[17] Arterburn, Stephen *et al*. <u>More Jesus Less Religion.</u> (Colorado Springs: Waterbook Press, 2000), p. xii.

[18] Magness, Lee. "Teaching and Learning in the Gospels: The Biblical Basis of Christian Education", *Religious Education 70*, no 6 (November-December, 1975, 629-35).

[19] Richards, Lawrence O. <u>Expository Dictionary of Bible Words</u>. (Grand Rapids: Zondervan, 1985), p. 591.

[20] Benson, Warren S. "Christ the Master Teacher" in <u>Christian Education: Foundations for the Future</u>. Robert E. Clark *et al, editors*. (Chicago: Moody Press, 1991), p. 89.

21 Edersheim, Alfred. *The Life and Times of Jesus the Messiah, 9th Print*. (US: Hendrickson Publishers, 2006), pp. 845-9.

22 Henry, Matthew. *Commentary on the Whole Bible*. (Peabody: Hendrickson, 1991), p. 2018.

23 Benson, Warren S. "Christ the Master Teacher" in *Christian Education: Foundations for the Future*. Robert E, Clark *et al, editors*. (Chicago: Moody Press, 1991), p. 87.

24 The Holy Bible. King James Version-A Reference Edition with Concordance, (New York: The American Bible Society, 1963).

25 Benson, Warren S. "Christ the Master Teacher" in *Christian Education: Foundations for the Future*, Robert Clark *et al, editors*. (Chicago: Moody Press, 1991), p. 87.

26 Carnegie, Dale. *How to Win Friends & Influence People*, *reprint*. (New York: New Pocket Book, 1981), pp. 89-90.

27 Fuller, Daniel P. *The Unity of the Bible.* (Grand Rapids: Zondervan, 1992), pp. 150, 255.

28 Greek *'Petra'*, means 'rock'.

[29] Jensen, Irving L. <u>Jensen's Survey of the New Testament</u>. (Chicago: Moody Press, 1981), p. 209.

[30] Parentheses are added for clarification.

[31] Gangel, Kenneth D. "What Christian Education Is", in <u>Christian Education: Foundations for the Future</u>, Robert Clark *et al*, editors. (Chicago: Moody Press, 1991), p. 22.

[32] Guthrie, Donald. "Jesus" in <u>A history of Religious Educators</u>, Elmer E. Towns, *ed*. (Grand Rapids: Baker, 1975), pp. 26-35.

[33] Jensen, Irving L. <u>Jensen's Survey of the New Testament</u>. (Chicago, Moody Press, 1991), p. 473.

[34] Edersheim, Alfred. <u>The Life and Times of Jesus the Messiah,</u> (US: Hendrickson Publishers, 2006), p. 833.

[35] Current Turkey

[36] *Pergamum* was the religious capital of the Romans and the center for four idol worships.

[37] *Nicolaitans* refers to an unknown group of heresy. Name means dictators or 'Children of Balaam'.

[38] The Holy Bible. King James Version. (American Bible Society: New York, 1963), p. 877.

[39] Arterburn, Stephen. *et al*. <u>More Jesus Less Religion</u> (Colorado Springs: Waterbook Press, 2000), p.150.

[40] Cloud. Henry *et al*. <u>How People Grow,</u> (Grand Rapids: Zondervan, 2001), p. 19.

[41] Warren, Rick. <u>God Power to Change Your Life</u>. (Grand Rapids: Zondervan, 2006), p. 74.

[42] Magness Lee. "Teaching and Learning in the Gospels": The Biblical Basis of Christian Education, *Religious Education 70*, no 6 (November-December 1975): 629-35.

[43] Benson, Warren S. "Christ the Master Teacher" in <u>Christian Education: Foundations for the Future</u>, Robert E. Clark *et al, editors*. (Chicago: Moody Press, 1991), p. 89.

[44] McKenna, David. <u>Power to Follow, Grace to Lead,</u> (FL: W Pub Group, 1989), pp. 124-5.

[45] Edersheim, Alfred. <u>The Life and Times of Jesus the Messiah</u>, 9th Printing. (US: Hendrickson Publishers, 2006), p. 833.

[46] A talent was worth more than a thousand dollars: The Holy Bible. New International Version. (Grand Rapids: Zondervan, 1983), p.759.

[47] The prophecy was fulfilled.

[48] Hughes, Philip E. *A Commentary on the Epistle to the Hebrews*. (Grand Rapids: Eerdmans, 1977), p. 385.

[49] Sproul, L. C. *The Last Days According to Jesus,* 7th ed. (Grand Rapids: Baker Books, 2007), pp. 131-149.

[50] Gentry, Kenneth L, Jr. *The Beast of Revelation.* (Tyler: Institute for Christian Economics, 1989).

General Index

Accomplished mission,..........156-164
   the end of the world,....160-61, 164
   Jesus as the Judge, ...159-60
   the kingdom of heaven
      parables,.......156, 159, 161, 164
   parable of the 'Talents', ...156-59
   parable of the 'Sheep and
      the Goats',...............100, 103, 156,
      159-60
   parable of the 'Ten Virgins',......156
Act(s), ...26, 33, 51, 56, 66, 71,
   110-11, 131-33, 154
Adam, ...15, 18, 21, 103, 158, 163
Adultery, ...54-5, 113, 137
Affiliation, ...95
Agony, ...42-3, 97
Ambassador, ... 145
Angel(s),
      ascended,.....................................52
      the devil and his,......................103
      the Father and His,...................136
      God's command to,....................51
      the host of, ...30
      of the Lord, ...29, 121-22
      to Mary,......................................97
      Son of Man and,................25, 159
Apocalypse, ... 161
Apostle(s),
      claimed to be,...........................136
      of Jesus,....................................124
      (John),..................17, 44, 96, 103,
         114, 131, 134-35, 137
      later called,..............................134

      (Luke),......................................132
      miracles of the,........................132
      (Paul), ...104, 131, 133
      teaching of the,........................150
Aramaic,...................................55, 65
Arrival,
   teaching on the kingdom,..........69
Arrogance, ...92
Arterburn, Stephen,...............66, 142,
   171, 174
Ascension,
   before Jesus', ...39, 41, 111,
   141, 151
   after Jesus', ...23, 37, 44,
   131, 154
Assurance,
   See blessed assurance
   blessings of, ...110, 112-16, 155
   of eternal life,..............................36
   faithfulness and,.............133, 157
   faith precedes, ...107-08, 110
   God's,...........82, 107, 109, 113-16
   having a strong,...............141, 157
   message of, ...83
   personal,....................................62
   privilege in Christian, ...111-12
   source of, ...36, 107, 109-11
Attitude,
   avoiding antagonistic, ...69
   creating a positive, ...19, 133, 142
   growth develops, ...142
   of the heart, ...160
   Jesus',........................38, 85, 104

low-key, ...76
ordinances and Jesus', ...85
Audience,
    auditory sense of the, ...108
    change lives of the, ...11
    format to convince, ...68
    Jesus', ...35
    mesmerize the, ...67
Authority,
    God's, ...58, 141, 148, 155
    He gave them, ...22, 136, 149
    spoke with, ...48, 67, 78
    taught with power and, ...11, 47-8

Bandit, ...43
Baptism, ...39
    baptize, ...149, 151, 155
Barrier, ...154
Bartimaeus, ...98
Beatitude(s), ...52, 68, 70-1
    format of, ...68, 70
    key-reminders of, ...71
Benson, Warren, ...34, 49, 52, 70, 92, 149, 169-72, 174
Blessed assurance,
    the aspect of worrying, ...108
    blessings of, ...112-16
    definition of, ...107
    privilege, ...111-12
    source, ...109-11
Branch, ...83, 88-90
Bread,
    breaking of the, ...32
    consecrated, ...77
    daily, ...58
    the flesh, ...75
    the living, ...31, 75
Buddhism, ...18
Burial, ...64, 105, 151

Change(s) (ed),
    See permanent change
    churches, ...135
    future, ...18

glorious, ...115
God's purpose for, ...24
instant, ...142
law, and, ...48
life, ...11, 24-5, 31, 66, 88, 115, 133, 145
permanent, ...86, 88-9, 93
physical and spiritual, ...64, 75, 93, 96, 102, 133, 143
Christ,
    after, ...46, 150
    before, ...46
    church of, ...86, 131-35, 152
    communion of, ...155
    the friend, ...86
    God sending His Son, ...28, 158
    growing into the
        likeness of, ...91, 147
    incarnation of, ...32
    Jesus, ...33, 45, 49, 83, 104, 134
    leading others to, ...26
    members of the body of, ...27, 83, 91, 133, 139
    mirror the holiness of, ...21
    model ministries after, ...26, 92
    never losing touch, ...70
    the person of, ...144
    reconciliation through, ...50
    redemption by, ...48-9, 141, 158
    second coming of, ...161-62
    selecting the twelve, ...34-5
    teaching ministry of, ...49, 84, 133, 152
    torture for the name of, ...41
Christian(s),
    assurance of, ...112-12
    as branches, ...89
    detachment of, from, ...71
    faith of, ...56, 60, 88, 141
    fellowship of, ...88, 131-33
    growth of, ...138, 141-42, 144
    Jesus likened good, ...54, 83
    life of, ...89, 92, 95-6, 133
    love of, ...17, 25, 55

ministry of, ... 133, 143
orthodox, ...33
peace fills the, ...39
the sanctity of, ...55, 70, 104, 138
the true, ...49, 87, 141-42, 145
Christianity,
converted to, ...96
defining bases of, ...56, 131, 160
fruit of, ...87
pillar of, ...147
Church(es),
birth of the, ...131
building Jesus', ...97, 101, 129-30
evaluating the seven, ... 135, 137, 162
first Christian, ...132-34, 152
giving assurance to the, ...114
initiation of the
  newborn, ...22, 129, 131
love among members of the, ...87-8
the present, ...144
unity of the, ...27, 134, 154
Cleanliness, ...84
Clean, ... 35, 83, 85, 88, 101, 111
unclean, ...35, 84, 86, 101, 154
Cleanse, ...89,92,
Commandment. 18, 23, 25, 27, 38, 50, 77, 85, 94-6, 113, 142
Communion, ...132-33, 154
Compassion,
for the disciples, ... 22, 39, 111
love and, ...98, 119
a man of, ... 17, 32, 39
Compassionate, ...31, 52
Completion, ... 158, 164
Confidence, ... 107, 110, 115
Confirmation, ...84
Content, ...76, 70
Continued fellowship,
the birth of the church, ...129-32
the churches of
  Asia Minor, ...135, 137
conditions of
  fellowships, ... 134, 144

the filling of the
  Holy Spirit, ...133-34
perception of the
  Father's kingdom, ... 129
Counter-question, ...73
Creation,
before the, ... 15, 16, 21
creation order, ...50
God's, ... 108, 158
love towards, ...16
process of, ...158
purpose in, ...21
since the, ...25, 103
Crucifixion, ...39, 41-3, 48, 64, 91, 105, 151
Day(s),
day and night, ...20, 59
forty, ...59
Judgment, of, ...156, 160-61
Last, ...65
the Lord, of, ... 160
Pentecost, of, ... 111, 131
three, ...30, 72
the third, ...41
Death,
arrest, trial and, ...41-3
on the cross, ...33
crucifixion and
  bleeding to, ... 100, 145
eternal, ...23, 37
giving himself to, ...100
murder and, ...55
obedient to, ... 104, 126
resurrection from, ...72
shadow of, ...29
victory over, ...41
on wages of sin and, ...26, 50
Defilement, ...84-5
Demon-possessed, ...32, 52, 98
Destruction, ...60, 160, 163
Devil, ...40, 51-2, 103, 140
Devotion, ...64, 87, 132

Disciple(s),
    the betrayer, ... 97
    the commission to the, ... 88, 129, 131,
        124, 141, 145, 148, 150-51, 155
    complaint against the, ... 77, 84-5
    conversation with the, ... 17, 33,
        50, 68
    entourage of, ... 34-5
    forgiveness of His, ... 99
    Jesus' comfort for the, ... 39,
        111, 113
    Jesus' compassion for the, ... 87
    Jesus' discerning love
        to His, ... 94, 99, 101
    Jesus the model teacher
        for the, ... 35, 59, 68-9, 104,
          110, 120, 130, 143, 147,
          152, 160
    obedience of the, ... 124
    outpour of the Holy Spirit
        to the, ... 22, 111, 150
    twelve designated, ... 34, 152
    union between Jesus
        and the, ... 20, 48, 97, 111, 134
    untraditional, ... 154-55
    washing the feet of the, ... 96,
        104, 129
Discourse, ... 50, 67, 82, 84,
    86-8, 91, 115, 152, 156, 159-60
Divorce, ... 54-5, 78

Edersheim, Alfred, ... 84, 134, 154
Education, ... 19, 147
    non-formal, ... 40, 65
Educational, ... 19
Egypt, ... 48
Elijah, ... 33, 130
Embodiment,
    of God, ... 21
    of joy, ... 21
    of Jesus, ... 92
    of love, ... 37
Encouragement, ... 82

End(s),
    endurance to the, ... 114
    friendship, never, ... 118
    government and peace
        without, ... 29
    judgment at the, ... 55
    love unto the, ... 96
    means to an, ... 47
    pre-end, ... 164
    quest, never, ... 92
    remain until the, ... 155
    second coming at the, ... 92
    victory at the, ... 51
    the world, ... 160-61
Ephesus, ... 114, 135
    Ephesians, ... 26
Ethic(s), ... 17, 23, 26, 69, 70-1, 119

Faith(s), ... 19, 33, 41, 56, 60, 70,
    72-3, 87-8, 96, 100, 107, 110,
    141-45, 150
Faithful, ... 35, 45, 115, 118,
    130, 136, 156, 160
Faithfulness, ... 33, 157
Fasting, ... 56, 59, 68, 78
Father(the)
    acknowledgement before, ... 136
    ascension to, ... 96, 155
    asking for forgiveness
        from, ... 97-9
    baptism in the
        name of, ... 129, 141, 148, 151
    being in the presence of, ... 136
    blessings of, ... 25, 103
    embodiment of joy of, ... 21
    the everlasting, ... 29
    fellowship with, ... 133-34
    the heavenly, ... 24, 38, 58, 61,
        95, 107-08, 120, 130
    the house of, ... 31
    Jesus, the way to, ... 31, 90
    the kingdom of the, ... 109, 111,
        115, 129

love of the, and
the Son, ... 17, 19-20
only the Son has seen, ... 17, 48
praying in the
name of, ... 58, 65, 90
reconciliation with, ... 50
redemption plan by, ... 133
relationship between
the Son and, ...87-9
the Son teaching about, ... 31,
47, 91, 117
submitting one's life to, ... 21
surrendering to the will of, ... 41-2,
48, 68
unity between the Son and, ... 22
Feet,
the guide for our, ... 29
pouring perfume on Jesus', ... 105
reaching down to his, ... 44
shaking the dust off one's, ... 149
trampling under the, ... 57, 140-41
washing the disciples', ... 96, 104,
120
Fellowship,
See continued fellowship
conditions of, ... 134
enjoying a rich,
with the Son, ... 101-2, 146
family and youth, ... 144, 146
man's duty to have, ... 91, 146
the Master's teaching on, ... 47
obstacles to continued, ... 137
role of the church
in continued, ... 129, 131, 146
role of the Holy Spirit in, ... 91
role of prayer in, ... 91
role of the Triune God in, ... 133-34
Fishermen, ... 124, 148
Fishing, ... 34, 125
Forgiveness
declaration of, ... 123
the Lord's, ... 58, 98, 122
message of love and, ... 39, 56, 58
teaching on, ... 33, 98, 144

Format(s),
of argument, ... 68
of beatitude, ... 68
different, ... 65
literary, ... 70
teaching, ... 51
Freidman, Matt, ... 22, 35
Friend(s),
See the matchless friend
matchless, ... 37, 117-18,
Abraham as, ... 122-23, 90
Jesus calls Christians, ... 86, 90, 117
privilege of having Jesus
as a, ... 118-19, 123
Friendship,
amazing facts
about Jesus', ... 118-24
conditions of, ... 117
joy of true, ... 117
Fuller, Daniel, ... 16, 120, 122

Galilee,
disciples' meeting
Jesus in, ... 97-8, 151
Jesus' walk beside
the Sea of, ... 48
springing from, ... 40, 63
Gangel, Kenneth, ... 132
Gardener,
the Father as the, ... 31, 72, 83, 88
Gate(s),
of Hades, ... 129-30
of heaven and hell, ... 60
I am the, ... 31
the narrow and wide, ... 60
Gentiles,
disciples' interaction
with the, ... 154
Jesus' ministry to the, ... 154
the Jews and the, ... 35-6, 134
ordinance on defilement
followed by the, ... 84
separating the Jews
from the, ... 85

Glory,
    God's power and, ...49, 58, 88
    God's satisfies His, ... 16
    heavenly, ... 25,159,
    host of angels sing, ... 30
    sinners falling short
        of God's, ... 49
    Solomon's, ... 60
    Son of Man returns in, ... 25, 159
Goat(s),
    parable of 'The Sheep and
        the Goats', ... 100, 103, 156,
        159- 60
Gospel(s), ... 35, 65-6, 68-9, 73,
    88, 90, 111, 129, 133, 147-53
    of John, ... 20-1, 30, 62-3, 75, 87
    of Luke, ... 29, 131
    of Mark, ... 17, 84, 86, 149
    of Matthew, ... 130
    the three synoptic
        gospels, ... 30, 160
Grace,
    freely justified by His, ... 49
    having the God of, ... 48
    inherit God's, ... 26
    living by God's, ... 49
    love out of mercy and, ... 16
    the need for, ... 49
    the role of truth and, ... 144
    salvation through, ... 93, 103
Grave(s),
    buried in a rich man's, ... 43
    hypocrites similar to
        unmarked, ... 71
Greek, ... 133, 172
Growth,
    See personal growth
    artificial. 139, 142
    Christian, ... 91,144, 147
    individual, ... 91, 144
    natural, ... 139
    obstacles to, ... 141
    personal, ... 147
    process of, ...91, 142-44

    spiritual, ... 91, 139-42, 144-47
    true, ... 142, 147
Guthrie, Donald, ... 47, 133

Hades, ... 129-30
Happiness,
    everlasting, ... 156, 164
    less assurance resulting
        in less, ... 109
    sharing God's supreme, ... 18,20,
        115, 159
Healing,
    act of, ... 51-2, 66
    miracles of, ... 52
    power of, ... 32
    process of physical
        and spiritual, ... 52, 76
    teaching through, ... 52,68,
        115, 150
    witnessing the
        miracles of, ... 66, 119
Heaven,
    ascension to, ... 22, 24, 41, 131
    assurance of eternal
        life in, ... 24, 36, 53, 56, 96,
        115, 130
    the fall of Satan from, ... 73
    the Father in, ... 24, 38, 58, 61,
        95, 99, 107-08, 120
    the gate to, ... 60
    God's supreme authority on earth
        and in, ... 25, 141, 148, 155
    Jesus' return from, ... 29, 31, 75
    kingdom of, ... 17, 25, 50, 53-4,
        70, 119, 130, 156, 159
    a new, ... 161
    a preview of, ... 25, 110, 159, 161
    rejoicing in, ... 38
Hell,
    condemned to, ... 40, 55
    eternal, ... 17, 23, 115
    the gate to, ... 60
    a preview of heaven and, ... 161
Herod, ...41

High Priest(s),
    Annas, the non-official, ... 42
    false accusations of the, ... 99
    turning Jesus over to the, ... 99
Hillel and Shammai, ... 84-5
Holy Spirit (the),
    anointment of, ... 33
    baptism of, ... 129
    of Comfort, ... 22, 41
    embodiment of joy of, ... 21
    existence of, ... 21-22
    the Father, the Son and, ... 21
    the filling of , ... 89, 91-2, 109
    fruit of, ... 90-1
    growth in, ... 139-41
    inspiration by, ... 44
    promise of the
       outpour of, ... 87, 111
    receivers of, ... 91-2
    of Truth, ... 87
    unity of church through, ... 133
Hope, ... 107, 110-11, 113, 146
Hughes, Philip, ... 160
Humankind,
    God's benevolent love to, ... 15, 52
    God's purpose to save, ... 18, 25-7
    greatest gift to, ... 117
    message of peace to all, ... 40
    sharing the gospel with all, ... 148
Hyperbole, ... 73
Hypocrite(s), ... 40, 58, 61, 78

I (am) the,
    gate, ... 31
    good shepherd, ... 31
    light of the world, ... 31
    living bread, ... 31
    Lord, ... 94
    true vine, ... 31
    way, the truth and the life, ... 31
Immorality, ... 92, 137
Incarnation, ... 32
Inspiration, ... 35

Inspire(d), ... 35, 44, 118, 153, 160, 163
Involvement, ... 144, 150
Isaac, ... 90, 123
Isaiah, ... 28, 78, 85, 146
Islam, ... 18, 160
Israel,
    God's nation, ... 16, 22, 106
    objectives for, ... 22
    the Roman Empire and, ... 34
    tribes of, ... 36
    the unrepentant, ... 74

Jensen, Irving, ... 16, 42, 131-32, 134, 163
Jesus,
    See the person of Jesus
    attitude towards sinners, ... 38
    becoming like, ... 25-6
    Christianity IS, ... 33
    embodiment of love, ... 37
    existence of, ... 30
    first-hand love for, ... 20
    Incarnate Son, ... 32
    Isaiah's prophecy on
       the birth of, ... 28
    John's revelation of, ... 44-6
    king, ... 34, 39
    man of compassion, ... 39
    man of fulfillment, ... 40
    man of justice, ... 36
    man of modesty, ... 37
    man of suffering, ... 41-4
    servant, ... 33
    teacher and rabbi, ... 34
Jews, ... 23-4, 35-6, 40, 67, 77, 85, 134, 138, 154, 161
Jezebel, ... 137
John,
    the Apostle, ... 17, 37, 44, 96, 101, 103, 115, 131
    the Baptist, ... 29, 33, 68, 130
    Gospel of, ... 20-1, 30, 33, 62, 75-7, 87

Epistle of, ... 134
Revelation of, ... 135, 161-63
Joy,
assurance resulting in, ... 113
embodiment of, ... 21
empowering Christians with, ... 90
enduring the cross with, ... 100
of friendship, ... 117
the fruit of the Spirit is, ... 133
increasing the, ... 16, 20, 125
in heaven, ... 24
perseverance develops, ... 145-6
reaping in, ... 73, 153
sharing the, ... 16, 18, 91, 117
spreading the gospel with, ... 133
of the Triune God, ... 17, 21, 25
Judas Iscariot, ... 97, 99
Judgment, ... 54-5, 156, 161
Justice, ... 19, 20, 29, 36, 59, 79, 99

Key(s), ... 16, 23, 71, 76, 91, 130, 133
King(s),
James, ... 96
the Lord as, ... 25, 33-4, 45, 103-4
of peace, ... 39
Xerxes, ... 23
Kingdom(s)
ethics of the, ... 17, 23, 26, 69
everlasting, ... 161, 164
of God, ... 17, 23, 29, 53, 58-9,
61-3, 67, 69, 71, 73, 76, 86, 109,
119, 129, 145
of heaven, ... 17, 50-1, 53, 70,
103, 115, 130, 156, 159
inheritance of the, ... 25, 145
made us, ... 45, 119
mysteries of the, ... 70
of the world, ... 51
Kuhlman, Edward, ... 48

Land,
of Egypt, ... 48
the promised, ... 16, 48, 78
Laodicea, ... 135

Law(s),
dying to the, ... 143
fulfillment of the, ... 20, 40-1,
54, 78, 92
God of the, ... 48
interpretation of the, ... 54-7,
63, 84, 86
judgment of the, ... 48, 55
summary of the, ... 19
teachers (teaching) of the, ... 32, 37,
47, 54, 67, 92, 150
Leader(s),
religious (Jewish), ... 35, 42,
62-4, 159
Leadership, ... 32, 152
Light,
ability to see the, ... 27, 120
bringing humankind to the, ... 134
Christians as the, ... 54, 121, 151
I am the, ... 31

Magness, Lee, ... 66, 147
Manager,
parable of the
'Dishonest Manager', ... 70
Manifestation, ... 133
Mark (Gospel of), ... 17, 18, 26, 42,
84, 86, 149
Market, ... 71, 85
Mary Magdalene, ... 97
Master plan, ... 148
The Master's teaching methods,
the beatitude, ... 52, 68, 70-1
literary and poetic
devices, ... 67, 71-5
the parable, ... 24, 59, 68-70, 74,
98, 100, 103, 111, 113, 115, 119,
129, 140, 156, 158-59
people's
interest in, ... 16, 35, 119-21
transformational
teaching, ... 74, 76-7, 91, 142, 144
the woe, ... 40, 53, 68, 70-1

The matchless friend,
   Abraham God's friend,.... 90, 122-3
   obedience, ... 17, 90, 123-24, 144
   privilege of Jesus'
      friendship, ... 118-19, 123, 145
   true friendship, ... 118
Message, ... 12, 15, 23, 38, 40,
   47, 50-2, 62, 67-9, 76, 83, 88, 92,
   108, 119, 135, 156
The message of the Master,
   on adultery, ... 54-5, 113, 137
   the beatitudes, ... 52, 68, 70-1
   Christian doctrines, ... 49-50, 56,
      75, 77, 132, 144
   on divorce, ... 54-5, 78
   on fasting, ... 56, 59, 68, 78
   on love, ... 15-23, 37-8
   to the tempter, ... 51-2
   on murder, ... 54-5, 92
   to Nicodemus, ... 62-4
   on prayer, ... 27, 57-9, 68,
      72, 91, 102, 115, 150
   on self diagnosis, ... 54
   on the teaching of
      the Law, ... 54-7, 63, 84, 86
   through healing, ... 32, 51-2,
      66, 76, 115, 119, 150
   the woes, ... 40, 53, 68, 70-1
Messiah,
   expectation by the Jews
      about the, ... 40, 109
   fulfillment of the prophecy
      about the, ... 16, 67
   God's plan for the, ... 16
   the true, ... 33, 109
Metaphor, ... 72, 141
Method(s), ... 15, 34-5, 47, 52,
   65-9, 76, 98
   See the Master's teaching methods
Ministry, ... 26-7, 31, 41, 49, 52,
   59, 69, 99, 133-34, 148, 150-53
Miracle(s),
   feeding the five thousand, ... 67
   healing, ... 32, 52, 98, 115

   incarnation, ... 32, 68
Mission, ... 41, 43-4, 48, 133, 150,
   154, 156, 158-9, 161, 164
   See accomplished mission
Multitudes, ... 49, 62, 86, 119
Murder, ... 54-5, 92
Mustard, ... 70, 73, 143

Nature, ... 60, 101, 104
Needy, ... 27, 52-7, 113
Neighbor, ... 18-19, 23, 38, 50, 76,
   94-5, 142, 158
Nicodemus, ... 62-4

Oath, ... 54-5
Obedience,
   Abraham's, ... 90, 122-23
   disciples', ... 124
   permanent connection
      through, ... 17, 90
   personal growth
      resulting from, ... 144
Offering, ... 27, 52-7, 113, 104
Ordinance(s), ... 84-6

Parable(s),
   the dishonest manager, ... 70
   the lost sheep, ... 24, 68, 154
   presenting the kingdom
      through, ... 69-70, 156
   the prodigal son, ... 74
   the sheep and the goats, ... 100,
      103, 156, 159
   the sower, ... 140
   the talents, ... 156, 158
   the true vine, ... 111, 113, 119
   the unmerciful servant, ... 98
   the virgins, ... 156
   the widow and the judge, ... 59
Parallelism, ... 71, 74
Passover, ... 34, 96
Peace,
   came to throw a
      sword, not, ... 39, 78

fruit of the Spirit and, ...40
a guide in path of, ... 29, 106, 114
increase of
   government and, ...29, 39
king of, ...39, 112
makers of, ...59, 114
message of, ...40
prince of, ...29
Pentecost, ... 111, 131
Pergamum, ... 135
Permanent change,
   the Father as the gardener
      of the vine, ...83, 88
   followers as the branches
      of the vine, ...83, 89
   friends of Jesus, ...86
   fruits of the Spirit, ...87, 89
   the Holy Spirit, ...87, 89
   the issue of defilement, ...84-5
   the Son as the true vine, ...83, 88
Perseverance, ... 135-36, 142, 145-46
Personal growth,
   characteristics of spiritual
      growth, ...141-43, 146
   obstacles to growth, ... 141
   parable of the 'Sower', ... 140
The person of Jesus,
   See the person of Jesus
   accepting, ...27
   attitude towards sinners, ...38
   becoming like, ...25-6
   Christianity IS, ...33
   embodiment of love, ...37
   existence of, ...30
   first-hand love for, ...20
   the Incarnate Son, ...32
   Isaiah's prophecy on
      the birth of, ...28
   John's revelation of, ...44-6
   the king, ...34, 39
   man of compassion, ...39
   man of fulfillment, ...40
   man of justice, ...36
   man of modesty, ...37

man of suffering, ...41-4
the servant, ...33
the teacher and rabbi, ...34
Pharisees, ...35, 37-8, 48, 54, 63,
   69-72, 77, 85, 99, 101, 142, 154
Philadelphia, ... 135
Pontius Pilate, ...42-3, 64
Power,
   anointed with Spirit and, ...33
   assurance and, ... 112
   Christian growth and, ...87, 141
   coming out of
      Gethsemane with, ...42
   God's supernatural, ...41, 49,
      58, 142
   the healing, ...32
   of the Holy Spirit, ...41, 49, 92,
      109-10, 133, 143, 154
   teaching with
      authority and, ...35, 49
Praise, ...58, 110, 120, 135
Prayer, ...57-8
   the Lord's Prayer, ...57-8
Prophet(s), ...15, 19, 28-9, 33, 41,
   53, 61-3, 65, 77, 106, 130, 137, 161-2
Proverb(s), ... 74, 118
Pun, ...73

Rabbi, ...77, 84-5, 92, 142
Redemption, ... 16, 23, 33, 44,
   49-50, 115, 133
   being on the
      mission for, ...44, 50, 13
   joy in creation and, ... 16
   sacrifice for, ...2, 33, 115
Repetition, ...75, 162
Reprimand, ... 120, 135, 137
Resurrection, ...39, 72, 98, 152, 164
   His crucifixion and, ...39, 72
Revelation, ...15
   Book of, ... 44-5, 114, 135, 161-63
Revenge, ...19, 23-4, 94
Riddle, ...73

Righteousness,
    blessings of, ... 100, 103, 156, 159
    kingdom of justice and, ... 29
    a model of, ... 54
    persecuted for, ... 53
    seeking His
        kingdom and, ... 61, 109, 145
    thirst and hunger for, ... 53
Roman Empire, ... 34, 40, 43, 64, 67, 69, 99, 135
Rule,
    the golden, ... 18-19, 26, 129
    Roman, ... 40, 99, 135
    giving authority to, ... 21, 136
Ruler(s),
    Jewish, ... 41
    of all nations, ... 44-5
    the rich, ... 112

Sabbath, ... 66, 77, 162
Sacrifice,
    Abraham's, ... 90, 123
    essence of new life and, ... 100, 152
    Esther's, ... 23
    God's desire for
        mercy, not, ... 74, 77, 79
    Jesus' love and, ... 23, 99, 120
    Nicodemus' loyalty and, ... 64
    perfect sinless, ... 23, 33, 100, 120
Salvation, ... 27, 29, 33, 92, 115, 125, 151
Samaritan, ... 68, 76, 109, 151-2
Sanhedrin, ... 42, 55
Sardis, ... 135
Satan, ... 31, 42, 51-2, 74, 135, 138
Satisfaction,
    fulfillment to God's, ... 110, 158-59
    God's creation and
        sense of, ... 158
    offering with, ... 110
Scribes, ... 35-6, 38, 43, 48, 84-6, 92, 97, 99, 101

Sermon (on the Mount), ... 38, 41, 49, 52, 67, 71, 74, 95, 107, 114, 120, 151
Servant(s),
    followers no longer
        called, ... 86, 117
    Israel, God's, ... 122
    Jesus came as a, ... 33, 48
    reward for a faithful, ... 157
    strategy of being a, ... 32, 104
    the 'Talent' parable, ... 156-58
    the 'Unmerciful Servant'
        parable, ... 98-9
Sharing the gospel,
    blessed assurance, ... 155
    commitment, ... 151
    the Great Commission, ... 155
    Jesus' commands, ... 149-50
    levels of endurance, ... 151-53
    the union and
        communion with Jesus, ... 154-55
Sheep,
    joy of finding the lost, ... 31, 154
    the 'Lost Sheep' parable, ... 24, 68
    obedience to the shepherd, ... 89
    the 'Sheep and the
        Goats' parable, ... 100, 103, 156
    the shepherd's
        sacrifice for the, ... 31, 43, 101
Shepherd, ... 24, 26, 31, 45, 101, 159
Simile, ... 61, 73
Simon Peter, ... 17, 33, 123-24, 130
Sinner(s),
    Jesus' love for, ... 19, 24, 36, 79, 102
    judgment for the
        believers and, ... 160
    the Master attracts
        believers and, ... 36
    the Master's attitude towards, ... 38
    the Savior's redemption
        for, ... 24, 38, 50, 79, 153,
    socializing with, ... 37, 66, 154
Smyrna, ... 135

Stein, Robert, ... 65
Style, ... 65, 71, 73, 89, 161
Synonym, ... 72, 74-5

Temple, ... 30, 32, 51, 63, 72, 74, 110, 132, 136
Temptation(s), ... 52, 58, 144
Tempter, ... 51-2
  See, Satan, devil
Testament
  New, ... 19, 33, 37, 70, 79, 102, 120, 133, 161
  Old, ... 15, 19, 23, 48, 70, 74, 78, 94-5, 98, 101, 103, 153, 162
Testimony, ... 91, 149, 154
Throne(s), ... 25, 29, 36-7, 45, 100, 135-36, 159
Thyatira, ... 135
Tradition, ... 66, 77, 84-6, 92, 154
Traditionalism, ... 84-5
Transformation,
  of life, ... 142
  physical, ... 76
  process of, ... 75, 142
  spiritual, ... 75-6, 91, 144
Treasure, ... 56, 110, 135
Trinity,
  in creation, ... 16
  the joy of sharing the, ... 16
  in redemption, ... 16
  the second person of the, ... 33
Triune, ... 17, 21, 25
Trust, ... 62, 84, 89, 92, 107, 109-10, 112, 118, 143
Truth, ... 23, 26, 31, 62-3, 68, 73, 77, 86-7, 90, 100, 110, 115, 134, 143-4, 150, 153

Understanding God's purpose for mankind
  God's objective, ... 22
  God's purpose, ... 16-20
  the Golden Rule, ... 18-20

Jesus' master plan, ... 23
  submitting to God's purpose, ... 24-5
Union, ... 134, 154

Victory,
  Jesus crushed Satan and won, ... 31, 51
  promise of, ... 135-6
Vine,
  branches of the, ... 83, 89
  fruit of the, ... 87, 113
  the message of love from the, ... 84
  remaining connected with the, ... 86, 88
  the true, ... 31, 72, 83, 86, 119
Virgin(s),
  born of a, ... 28-9
  the 'Ten Virgins' parable, ... 156

Warning, ... 135, 137-38
Water(s),
  deep, ... 123
  the living, ... 76, 83
  the Samaritan's need for, ... 76
  sound of rushing, ... 44
  the Spirit hovering over the, ... 22
Widow,
  the 'Widow and the Judge' parable, ... 59
  the offering of the poor, ... 109-10
Woe(s), ... 40, 53, 68, 70-1
Word,
  in the beginning was the, ... 21
  feeding from God's, ... 83-4, 88, 90
  of God, ... 45
  He never said a, ... 43
  spreading the, ... 54, 124, 134, 152, 160
World,
  carrying the sins of the, ... 75
  creation of the, ... 15-16, 25
  effect of disciple

    selection on the, ... 34-5, 111,
        113, 129-34
    effect of incarnation on the, ... 32
    end of the, ... 34, 71, 96
    God's love to the, ... 25, 38
    joy and peace to the, ... 39
    spreading the Word to the, ... 54
        124, 134, 152, 160
    victory over the, ... 106, 114

Xerxes (king), ... 23